Don't Drive Like This™

Story-filled illustrations, limericks, and discussion prompts to help people become better, kinder drivers. Suitable for student drivers, new drivers, and experienced drivers.

For the sake of our families and communities, let's ensure that we...

Don't Drive Like an Ash™

Published by:
gd-insights, LLC
Post Office Box 21
Brookline, New Hampshire 03033 USA
gdietz@garydietz.com

Other works by Gary Dietz:

- *Dads of Disability: Stories for, by, and about fathers of children who experience disability (and the women who love them)*
  at www.dadsofdisability.com
- Product Marketing, Entrepreneurial work on LinkedIn
  at https://www.linkedin.com/in/garymdietz/

Disclaimers

Driving rules, regulations, and laws: The author and/or their agents (a) have made reasonable attempts to represent current generalized US driving rules accurately but make no warranty of the accuracy or applicability of the rules, laws, and/or recommendations represented in these materials in your state, province, city, or jurisdiction (b) take no responsibility for errors other than, when notified, to publish addenda on the web site or updates in future print editions. Please check with your local, regional, and/or state or provincial authorities if you are concerned about the validity of a specific rule, law, or driving suggestion referenced or applied in the writing or illustrations in these materials.

Health and behavioral discussions: No suggestions the author makes about stress or anger reduction should be considered professional medical or mental health advice. Please seek or recommend professional medical or mental health care if you believe you or the drivers you are training or trying to influence have mental health and/or anger issues that you, student drivers, family, peers, or student circles believe may impact your or their driving safety or the safety of the community.

Edition:

- July 2025, version 1.00

ISBN: 979-8-218-73343-8

gd-insights, LLC 001.1

Situations & Discussion Prompts

Root Causes & Avoidance Techniques

Detail from *The Stressed Out Student Driver*, page 88.

About This Project

Too many of us encounter aggressive behavior on the road. Sometimes we are on the receiving end of the behavior and, let's be honest, sometimes we are the driver being aggressive. Do you have a child, spouse, or friend who needs to learn how to manage their aggression? Do they need to explore how to calm down and not "lose it" in a vehicle?

Drivers can exhibit unsafe behaviors for various reasons:

- They may have forgotten the rules of the road. Or never learned them properly.
- They may have observed unsafe driving practices from role models starting as early as when they were young children.
- They sometimes knowingly act recklessly to attempt to save time.
- Daily frustrations or anger can be emotionally misdirected and lead to unsafe attitudes and behaviors behind the wheel.

In some cases, all these factors may be at play simultaneously.

The Numbers Are Alarming

Road rage incidents have surged by 500% over the past decade. According to a 2025 survey, millennial drivers (now aged ~28 to ~42) reported the highest rates of road rage behaviors:

- 51% admitted to honking aggressively.
- 46% yelled or cursed at other drivers.
- 36% made angry gestures.
- 32% drove 15 mph or more over the speed limit.

These statistics highlight the widespread prevalence of aggressive driving, underscoring the need for intervention among current drivers and improved training and preparation for new ones.

None of Us Are Immune

The genesis of this collection stems from my journey to address the impatience and frustration I experience while driving. Earlier in my life, my lack of patience led to bad driving habits, fortunately, and luckily, with no resulting collisions. Caring individuals helped me learn techniques to manage stress and impatience, which transformed my approach to managing my emotions and driving better and more safely.

While none of us are perfect drivers—I am certainly not—everyone can work on self-awareness and improvement. This collection aims to help drivers identify and choose safer, more legal, and kinder options in everyday road situations through humor, illustrations, and discussion. It also offers starting points to help you reduce or avoid unsafe decisions and road rage.

How Can We Facilitate Better Driver Behavior?
This project combines humor, visuals, and conversation prompts to help make our roads safer while fostering thoughtful reflection among drivers of all experience levels. This collection is designed for experienced drivers or for use by parents and professional driver educators to facilitate reflection and discussion for new drivers. These materials can be part of a multifaceted approach:

1. **Education:** Share real-world situations to reinforce the rules you already teach, and encourage drivers to reflect on current habits.
2. **Awareness:** Help drivers recognize emotional states that may lead to unsafe actions and interactions.
3. **Support Systems:** Using humor and story-based illustrations, instructors, parents, and peers can add context to sometimes "dry" driver manuals to increase discussion, engagement, and retention.

This project is designed for anyone seeking to improve their driving habits, whether they are new or seasoned drivers.

Why This Format?
Humor and visuals are powerful tools for learning. Research shows that visuals improve information retention by up to 400%. Humor significantly boosts recall because it encourages engagement. The story-driven illustrations in this book intentionally exaggerate examples to stimulate reflection and learn from others' mistakes.

What this volume isn't
This volume is not a driver's manual like the one you might have received from your local authorities or driver education instructor. It doesn't provide a complete set of rules and regulations, nor does it cover every situation a driver may face.

Instead, this volume focuses on common aggressive and dangerous scenarios that can be generalized. This collection encourages discussion and reflection among drivers, their peers, families, and instructors.

This volume doesn't provide answers! That's intentional. This volume isn't meant to be a set of reference materials. Instead, it was designed to support individual, group, and family learning and improve retention through humor, visuals, and discussion.

The expectation is that learners, new drivers, and experienced drivers will seek out the correct answers to challenges presented within the discussion prompts. Sources may include formal driver manuals, other relevant materials, or approved websites. And of course, peers, instructors, parents, and guardians. Note that "correct" answers may vary across jurisdictions, but the core anti-aggression lessons are universal.

Aren't "Ashford and Ashley" Illustrations Over-the-Top?

Perhaps, although some instructors might feel they are not edgy enough! The play on words, "Don't Drive Like an Ash," aims to be memorable without being too offensive. By showing what not to do, learners are encouraged to think carefully about their behaviors.

The approach in this collection combines them with thoughtful discussion prompts, fostering a balance of humility and practical improvement. This volume promotes positive reinforcement through:

- **Conversation and thought or writing prompts:** Each chapter includes prompts designed for personal reflection or to support group discussions about safe responses in difficult situations.
- **Use alongside other driving materials and instructions:** Refer to the visuals and discussion prompts in this collection, as well as formal materials from different sources, to prepare for and during class or other learning sessions. Driver license authorities and schools provide state-approved materials, online driving guidelines, and information about laws in your jurisdiction.
- **Incentives:** Safe driving often leads to rewards, such as reduced insurance premiums or fewer restrictions on licenses and parental controls for new drivers, when specific milestones are achieved.

Why These Specific Examples?

This volume features original illustrations and discussion prompts, informed by feedback from driving instructors, parents, and social media discussions. Although other examples exist, these were selected for their everyday relevance and practical applications in situations beyond those discussed.

Do you have suggestions for future editions? Contact us through **https://www.dontdrivelikethis.com**

Other *Don't Drive Like This* program content and offers
Please visit the website to get the latest news about this content, updates, and to learn about other materials and offerings as they become available.

This has been a passion project. Our goal is to improve safety for me, my loved ones, for you and your loved ones, and for all of our communities.

Be safe and calm out there.

Gary Dietz

Why Aggressive Driving?
How Do We Avoid It?

What is road rage? What is aggressive driving?

Road rage, a severe form of aggressive driving, is dangerous, illegal, and impairs safe and effective travel. These terms are closely related. For this material, we refer to "aggressive drivers" as those who engage in excessively unsafe and often illegal driving actions, and "road ragers" as individuals who elevate the emotional level and increase verbal or physical actions beyond those of mere aggressive drivers. In these materials, we use these terms somewhat interchangeably, as in many real-world situations, aggressive driving can lead to road rage or provoke road rage in others.

Impact and distress

Aggressive driving can harm both drivers and their passengers, especially children. It also affects other drivers, pedestrians, bicyclists, and bystanders. Sometimes they are indirectly impacted or literally impacted when an aggressive driver causes a collision.

Troubling statistics

Search for "road rage" or "aggressive driving" on the internet, and you'll find daily reports of statistics and current news stories about specific incidents that caused harm. A quick search recently showed that 80% of US drivers have experienced road rage or aggressive driving firsthand (according to Nextbase). In the US in 2023, road rage led to 481 shootings, and between 2014 and 2024, it caused 777 deaths (according to thetrace.org). Additionally, 17% of drivers regularly engage in aggressive behaviors, according to a recent AAA traffic safety culture index.

After rage

Adverse effects can persist even after aggression ends. Consider injuries, emotional recovery, increased insurance rates, citations (tickets), arrests, legal costs, time spent on auto repairs, and the impact that aggression can have on your and your family's brains, moods, and bodies. Additionally, consider fatalities caused by collisions—and high blood pressure. People don't say "you're going to give yourself a stroke" for no reason!

What causes aggressive driving?

Road rage can arise from many different factors. Both new and experienced drivers should take time to reflect on themselves and review the content in this book (and other sources) to discuss with peers, instructors, and parents. Recognizing these factors can help you prevent dangerous behaviors from becoming habits. Throughout these materials, there are brief explorations of different root causes of aggression and some avoidance techniques to reduce its impact when others display aggression.

Techniques to avoid aggressive driving

Learning to control your emotions and stay calm while driving is key for your safety, your passengers, and others around you. There are several techniques to reduce the risk of road rage or escalating situations caused by others' inappropriate behavior.

You don't just want to arrive; you want to arrive safely and with minimal stress. By understanding and discussing the situations in these materials and applying some or all of the techniques covered, you can develop an attitude and mindset that encourage a safe and enjoyable driving experience for yourself and everyone around you. Handling situations that can trigger road rage becomes easier the more you prepare yourself. Your efforts create a safer driving environment for you and others on the road.

Please read the health and behavioral discussions disclaimer on the copyright page of this book. Do not take any advice discussed here or elsewhere without consulting a guardian (if you are a minor) and/or a trusted medical or behavioral health professional.

Your task

As you read and discuss these and other materials, and have conversations about becoming a better, safer, calmer driver:

- Identify other **root causes** of aggressive driving and road rage.
- Identify and share additional **avoidance techniques**.
- Discuss the situations and your reflections. Figure out which avoidance techniques will work best for you and your personality type.

Please learn, discuss, and Don't Drive Like an Ash!™.

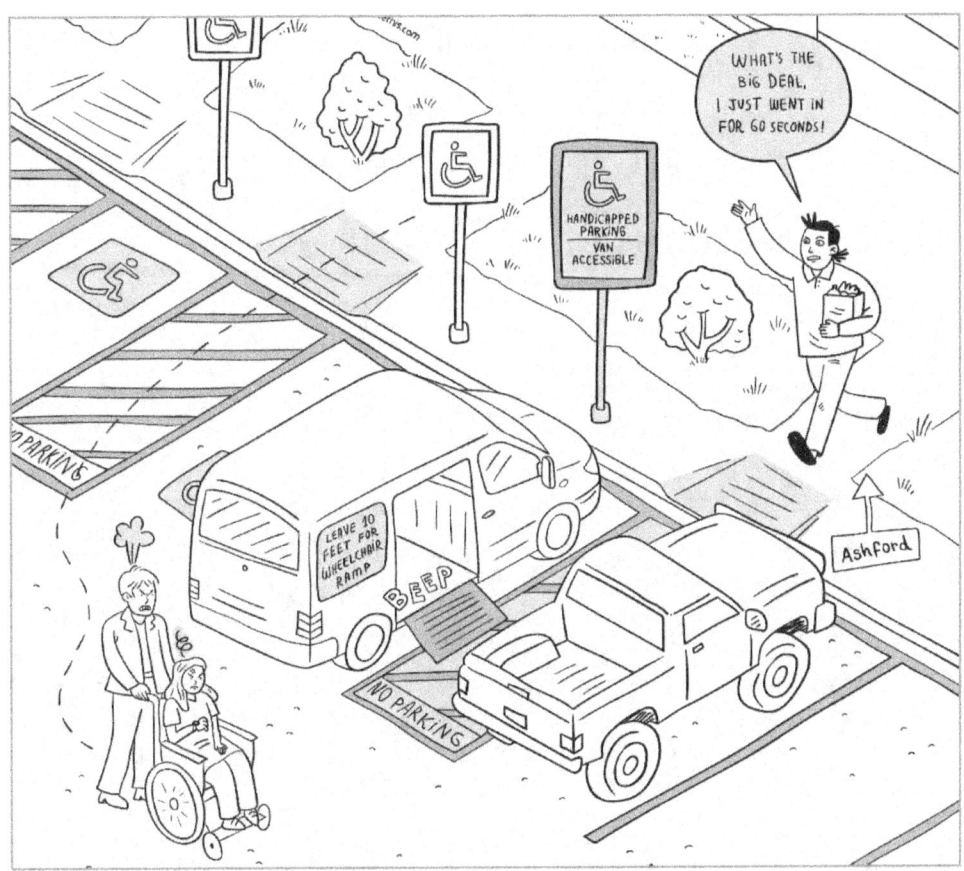

Detail from *The Abrasive Accessibility Abuser*, from page 94.
one of the ideas that started it all.

The No Right on Red Rager

Red light! Properly stopped in my lane.
Behind me, Ash is acting insane.
"No right turn," I obeyed,
Ash's tantrum displayed,
For road safety is not in his vein.

Ashford overlooks several important things. Can you identify them?

Things to think about, write about, or discuss

a) What things do you see that make a right on red in these conditions unsafe or illegal?

b) What things, perhaps not directly visible in this illustration, could be a safety issue when turning right on red when not allowed?

c) What regulations would you be breaking if you responded to Ashford's anger and made a right turn on red this very moment?

d) Are you ever **required** to make a right turn on a red light? What can happen if it is legal and safe to make a right on red, but you don't?

e) Do all jurisdictions have a legal right turn on red?

f) Is it your responsibility to teach Ash a lesson in any way? Should you scream back? Use aggressive hand gestures? Wait an extra 10 seconds to turn when the light turns green? Exit your car at the red light to calmly explain the correct action to Ashford?

g) If you've ever felt like Ashford does or acted like Ashford is acting now—c'mon, be honest—what are some things you could tell yourself or do in the moment to calm down?

h) What are some strategies you can use beforehand to prepare for others' possible anger at a red light where you can't turn because it's unsafe or illegal, whether or not the rager understands the situation?

i) Is it the responsibility of other drivers to break the law or drive unsafely to overcome Ashford's ignoring common-sense safety, traffic laws, and posted signs?

j) Does a traffic light and a decision on a right turn on red deserve as much attention as other "moving" vehicle situations?

The Troubling Testy Tailgater

Wipers on high and knuckles of white,
Ashford raged out, "This bozo's some sight!"
Very close with high beams,
His blood pressure extreme,
Risked a crash in the foggy twilight.

The weather isn't great, and this overpass has many curves and is quite windy. Ashford seems to be up to something and, as usual, is pretty angry.

Things to think about, write about, or discuss

a) The car in front of Ashford appears to be exceeding the speed limit. Is that acceptable in these conditions? Or is he going over the limit because of Ashford, and if so, is that okay?

a) Good practice and regulations sometimes require adjusting your driving based on weather and road conditions. What are some of the conditions that this illustration directly shows us?

b) What other road and weather conditions might you infer from this illustration that are not immediately obvious?

c) What dangers are Ashford creating for himself in this illustration?

d) How are the other cars in this picture, along with the ones likely soon coming into view, affected by Ashford's impatience and tailgating?

e) Given the extenuating circumstances in this situation, does the car in front of Ashford have the right or obligation to "brake check" Ashford to make him back up? Why or why not?

f) Given the extenuating circumstances in this situation, would it be better for the car in front of Ashford to just speed up by another 5 or 10 MPH?

g) Suppose there's a spot where the car in front of Ashford can safely pull over to let Ashford pass. Is it worth the trouble or extra time to do so to avoid the risks posed by Ashford? Or should the car in front simply ignore Ashford and continue as they normally would?

Root cause: Existing Personal Stressors

Unmanaged stress and frustration can cause road rage. If you experience high levels of stress at work, school, or home life, you could be prone to aggressive road behavior.

Each of us has natural levels of daily stress, although some days feel unnatural! When we get into a vehicle, our stress travels with us. Then, add traffic delays, congestion, inconsiderate drivers, bad weather, other drivers who may not react as quickly or as knowledgeably about your area, and tight schedules.

Ughhh! Aren't you stressing just thinking about it!

Unmanaged stressors brought into a vehicle can cause dangerous emotional overload while driving. And that results in... well, you know what that can lead to. Most of us have experienced it directed toward us firsthand.

And too many of us have been the aggressors. If you've been there, I'm glad you're reading this because it means you're alive and have the chance to grow and improve your driving behaviors, even during stressful times in your life.

Root causes and avoidance techniques discussed in this book can help you better handle your personal stressors, potentially reducing your aggressive tendencies and preparing you to avoid and manage them when others display similar behaviors.

As a lifelong learner, you should try to learn more about other root causes and avoidance techniques not discussed in these materials.

The School Bus Scofflaw

Ashley sped down a four-lane divide,
School Bus flashed STOP, but did Ash abide?
Kids dashed fast, left and right,
Ashley braked hard, such fright!
Cars behind skidded, honked, and some cried.

When a school bus is nearby, it's always safer to act conservatively. This applies whether you're a parent or an older student helping younger children board and leave the bus. As a driver, stay aware of all the rules in your area, and remember that many motorists don't know all the rules (even the most obvious ones), or if they do, they often fail to follow them.

Things to think about, write about, or discuss

a) Why might the cyclist in this illustration think they are not subject to school bus rules?

b) Why might Ashley have believed she could proceed at this moment? Why was she wrong?

c) Ashley eventually stopped, aligned with the "front" of the bus across the road. What characteristics about her "stop" are incorrect?

d) What might the cars behind Ashley have done differently?

e) If the car behind Ashley hit her, who would be responsible for the collision?

f) Describe a different roadway construction, but still two lanes in each direction, where Ashley could have proceeded legally? (That is, if there were no pedestrians she was in danger of colliding with.)

g) Why do you think Ashley ignored the small child running away from her mom, seemingly out of control? What extra precautions should Ashley (and everyone) take during school bus transportation hours?

h) How should overcast weather conditions in this illustration, or any other weather conditions, influence Ashley's actions during school bus transportation hours?

i) What street signs could be added to this neighborhood to help drivers avoid situations like this?

The Spontaneous Street Stopper

Ash braked in the play zone without flair,
To chatter with his friends, unaware.
The parent just behind,
Quickly braked in a bind.
Now his coffee is flying midair.

This illustration highlights many areas where attention is key. What should you be aware of when driving in places like this?

Things to think about, write about, or discuss

a) If there were no "Children at Play" signs on this part of the street, how would you modify your driving behavior?

b) Ashford makes a complete stop in the middle of an active road. What issues are there with this decision?

c) Based on this illustration, what could the car that screeched to a halt in the crosswalk have done differently, if anything? Assume that this car was not speeding.

d) Assume the car that screeched to a halt behind Ashford was not speeding. What actions should the driver behind Ashford have taken so it wouldn't have had to screech to a halt? Or was there no other option for that car, and the skidding stop was all Ashford's fault?

e) In your town, what are the usual speed limits on roads that run next to or cross a public park or playground?

f) Discuss each person's responsibility, including each driver, for any collisions or injuries that may have occurred if timings or speeds had been slightly different than what's currently shown.

g) In your opinion, how would speed bumps or other barriers on the road dividing the playground affect the safety of pedestrians and drivers in this illustration?

h) In your jurisdiction, what are the rules about stopping at a marked crosswalk when no explicit stop sign is present?

The Threatened Tractor Trailer

Ashton zipped past, then slowed down his pace,
Ashford nearing the blind spot's embrace.
Ashley drifted so near,
The close call was quite clear
Now this highway's a dangerous place.

Large trucks are common on many roads. Too often, drivers near them don't consider the truck's size, speed, weight, stopping distance, and blind spots.

Things to think about, write about, or discuss

a) Road conditions and weather should always influence your safety approach. Why are they especially important when driving near a large truck?

b) Ashford is passing this truck on the right. What danger is he and the truck driver in because of this decision, and what could he have done instead?

c) What is Ashley doing so close to the truck, and is she right to do it? Describe her visibility and the truck's visibility with regard to her.

d) Ashton passed the truck in the left lane. Describe the speed choices he made at each point, whether they were safe, and if there were safer options, how he could have handled the situation differently.

e) Describe what you believe the truck driver's stresses are in this situation. Is there anything the truck driver can do to improve his safety and/or the safety of others nearby?

f) If you haven't mentioned weather conditions yet, reflect on these discussion prompts, carefully considering the weather.
   1. How would your responses to the points above differ if it were snowing?
   2. If it was dark?
   3. If it was icy and dark?

g) What stressors do truck drivers face that differ from passenger car drivers, and how can you create safer conditions around trucks?

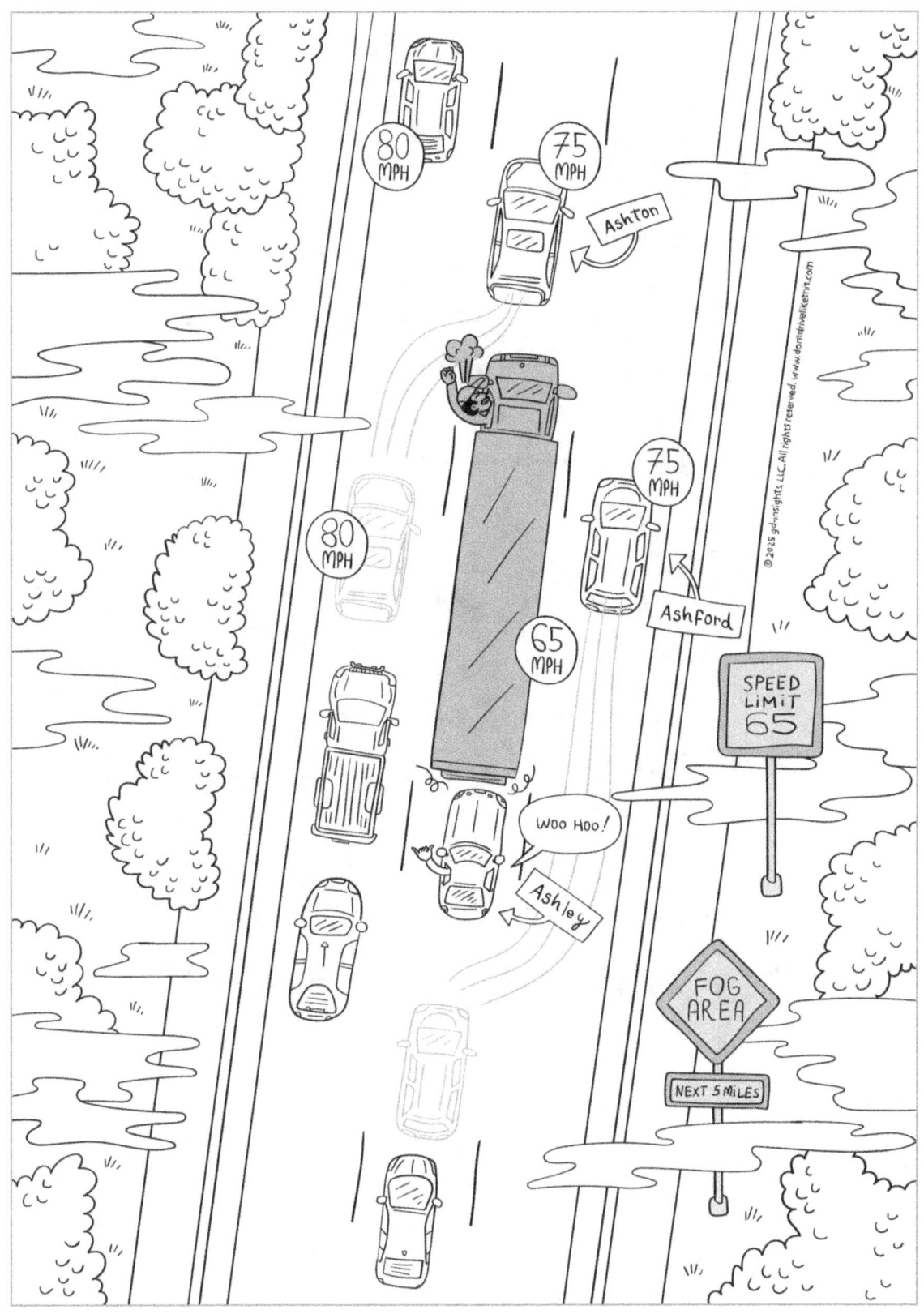

Avoidance Technique: Preparation and Planning

Before beginning a trip in your vehicle, no matter how brief, prepare yourself for success.

Give yourself extra time on your trip to prevent feeling rushed or stressed because of possible delays. Having a buffer of extra time can greatly lessen anxiety and frustration when you face unexpected traffic or road issues.

Make sure you're well-rested before driving. Drowsiness can cause impatience and aggression.

Take a few deep breaths after sitting in the vehicle and before starting it.

If something recently happened that causes stress or makes it hard to focus, consider waiting a while before driving. If you can't postpone the trip, take a few minutes to breathe deeply, reflect, and put your stressors "on hold" as best as you can.

There are many ways to prepare for a relaxed trip. Is prayer your thing? Meditation? A nice cup of herbal tea before heading into rush hour? A "mantra" repeated, telling yourself it will be a hard drive and that you commit to remaining calm?

What are some other ways to prepare and plan for a safe trip? What has worked for you? What new approaches could you try to see if they work just as well or better?

The Careless Crosswalk Killer

Ash's attention here was quite slim.
After all, the walk signs weren't dim.
Mom screamed loudly, so shocked,
Ash braked hard; Her car rocked!
The scene moments from turning quite grim.

Ashley overlooks clear signals in her environment and fails to ask herself fundamental questions. Traffic is halted ahead, yet she attempts to save time by swerving around the cars in front of her.

Things to think about, write about, or discuss

a) What environmental cues did Ashley overlook in this scenario?

b) Describe the safety of the skateboarder and his responsibilities.

c) If the car at the bottom of the page is fully stopped, is it okay for Ashley to swerve past if she had been driving at a safer speed and not been in a rage?

d) Are any pedestrians on the sidewalks at risk from Ashley's driving, and if so, how?

e) Imagine a situation where there is no designated pedestrian crosswalk on a four-lane road with two lanes in each direction.
   1. If traffic stops in one lane, how do you determine if passing the cars in that lane is safe?
   2. What warning signs might appear in an area without a pedestrian crossing that should make you extra cautious?

f) Describe dangerous, pedestrian-heavy areas in your community where you can request local authorities to install a crosswalk or blinking pedestrian crossing signal.

g) What might have happened if, under these conditions, Ashley had been playing her radio very loud or illegally wearing headphones or earbuds while driving?

The Miserable Motorcycle Muddle

Three lanes packed tight in the heat of day,
Motorcycles and cars in a fray.
Ashford's tailgating close,
Ashley loud and verbose.
Cars cause mayhem; Yet bikes sometimes stray!

Motorcycles are part of our transportation system whether you ride one or not. Motorcyclists need to be extra cautious because drivers of larger vehicles might not always be aware of the rules or conditions to keep everyone safe. However, sometimes motorcyclists are also to blame. All drivers of all vehicles must share the roads responsibly!

Things to think about, write about, or discuss

a) In some areas, "splitting the lane" is completely legal when done safely. It seems Ashley isn't aware that it's legal here. Explain the risks to the motorcycle, to Ashley, and to others nearby due to Ashley's lack of knowledge and awareness.

b) At the same time, Ashford is tailgating the motorcyclist ahead of him. What do you think Ashley understands about motorcycle braking distances? Airflow? blocking the visibility of the bike to other cars and trucks? What else should he know, and how should he be applying that knowledge in practice?

c) Not all motorcyclists in this illustration are at risk from car drivers. Up ahead, motorcyclists Ashwell and Ashwa are creating a less-than-safe situation themselves.
   1. Is it legal to "lane share" (ride two abreast) in all jurisdictions? In yours? Under what conditions? In what situations?
   2. Even if lane sharing is legal, what extra safety concerns might motorcyclists face or need to be aware of?
   3. What dangers do Ashwell and Ashwa face by following too closely behind the car in front of them? Are there extra tailgating risks because they are on a 65mph road where traffic is moving much slower than the speed limit?

The Loathsome Litterbug

Ashley sped down the road with a sneer,
Tossing butts with her passenger near.
Ashford blared his loud tunes,
Flung bags, bottles, and spoons.
While some ducks mourned the trash and a peer.

Tossing trash out of your window is gross, but it can also be dangerous. Even if you don't care about the environment (but you should!), trash tossing can cause problems for you and others.

Things to think about, write about, or discuss

a) What ways can different kinds of trash pose dangers to the car directly behind Ashford? Consider its weight, how hard it is, the speeds of the vehicles, if the trash will bounce, and other related issues.

b) How can throwing trash affect cars on the other side of the road?

c) What other risks does tossing cigarettes out of a car window pose besides the obvious fire hazard?

d) Littering on the roads usually results in a citation in most jurisdictions. What are the citation amounts in the areas you drive?

e) If your passenger(s) toss trash out of the window and a citation is issued, who can be held responsible for the citation in your jurisdiction?

f) If it is a jurisdiction where the driver can indicate it was the passenger who littered when a citation is issued, and you were the driver, how could this impact your relationship with the passenger?

g) What kinds of impacts do different types of litter have on an urban, rural, or suburban landscape?

h) If you see someone littering from their car, do you have any recourse?

i) When people in vehicles go beyond simple littering (such as food containers, bottles, cans, etc.) and actually "dump" large bags of trash, old appliances, or big objects on the side of the road (or off-road), what kinds of serious consequences could they face in your jurisdiction?

ROOT CAUSES OF AGGRESSIVE DRIVING

What other reasons can you identify?

Root cause: Misunderstood Intentions

Drivers who become angry may believe other drivers are "out to get them."

They may see others' honest mistakes as malicious or believe that other drivers are threatening their manhood, womanhood, or intentionally provoking them, even when that's not the case.

Negative assumptions about intentions can lead to faster and more unreasonable angry and aggressive driving responses.

Have you ever thought somebody was "up to something" in their car, but later realized it was a clever or safe move they were making based on conditions or a situation? Something you might have done yourself had you been able to see why they were doing it? For example, something as simple as someone pulling over quickly because they saw or heard an emergency vehicle before you did, or swerving right because they saw a pothole while you thought they were texting or drunk.

Always prioritize safety, but avoid rushing to judge and let your "lizard brain" react instantly. Take a moment to pause and reflect before responding emotionally or reacting.

The Lane Leaping Lunatic

With the top down and hair in the breeze,
Ash sped to cut off two cars with ease.
A hard left with a roar,
Left two cars wanting more:
Safety, serenity... and her keys!

Ashley is driving a sports car and is indeed "merging" into traffic.

Things to think about, write about, or discuss

a) Describe the actions Ashley took during her merge from the off-ramp that were illegal, unsafe, or both.

b) Describe the steps Ashley should have taken to merge onto the highway with the other cars, which are roughly in the positions shown in the drawing, assuming that the cars were traveling at the speed limit or slightly above.

c) Discuss what you think Ashley's focus was in the story that this illustration shows. Did anything in your interpretation of her thought processes bother you, and why? Why not?

d) What are some dangers Ashley exposed herself to by merging this way?

e) What are some dangers Ashley caused for other drivers by merging this way?

f) Is it a legal responsibility, a "shared responsibility," or simply a courtesy for cars already on the highway to adjust their speed and lane position to allow a car merging into traffic?

g) If it can be done safely, when should a car already on the main highway accommodate a vehicle entering the highway?

h) If a merging car collides with a vehicle already in traffic, and the vehicle that was already in traffic was driving safely and at a proper speed, in most cases, who would be responsible for the collision?

i) In this situation, what actions should other vehicles take to intentionally block Ashley or accelerate to punish her behavior, speed, or vehicle position?

The Lane Leaping Lunatic

39

The Bloody, Bambi Blunder

Ash tailgates past the deer crossing sign,
He's late! Deer nor turtles cross his mind.
Doe eyes shine in the dark,
Ashford's focus is stark.
Soon a screech, and the night's redefined.

Ashford and another car are on a rural or suburban road at night. This doesn't change the rules of the road, of course. If anything, the conditions should make us double down on many things.

Things to think about, write about, or discuss

a) What kind of time gap between cars driving at night should be added to what you would typically use during the day?

b) What other situational conditions on this rural road, or other types of roads, should you consider as you adjust your nighttime gap?

c) There isn't a posted speed limit sign, at least that we can see right now. If that's the case, what would the speed limit be and why?

d) The car ahead of Ashford was probably already moving slowly. Why?

e) What cues is Ashford missing generally, and what cues is he missing because he was tailgating the car in front of him?

f) Could anger or frustration be playing a role in the decreased situational focus Ashford is exhibiting?

g) What are some reasons that Ashford might not have passed, even though this section of the road is marked for passing?

h) When you see a deer crossing or leaping in the road, what are the key actions you should take for maximum safety? Do you follow this rule for other animals like rabbits, dogs, turtles, or larger mammals if they are in your area?

i) Describe if and how you would change your awareness and actions for animal crossings if this road were a major highway or an urban or suburban road with many household pets.

Avoidance Technique: Self-Care

Keep your overall stress levels in check, as they can affect your driving behavior.

Avoid driving when you're upset or dealing with stressful feelings.

Regular exercise or physical activity helps reduce overall stress.

Some people who practice mindfulness or meditation say it improves their overall emotional control. Studies have confirmed these results for some.

Some people who practice prayer say it helps them improve their overall emotional regulation. Studies have confirmed these results for some.

It sounds odd, but not taking bathroom breaks when you need them can cause stress and distract you.

The same for proper nutrition. Not eating enough or overeating can cause discomfort and distraction, which can lead to stress that may impact driving.

The Belligerent Brake Check

Two-lane highway, Ash sped with a sneer,
Passed the car though the stripes were quite clear.
At the sign, slammed her brakes,
Acted like a big flake
The safe driver behind shakes with fear!

In this illustration, the speed limit is higher before the drivers reach this situation. We see the sign warning of a slowdown ahead.

Things to think about, write about, or discuss

a) Assume the prevailing speed was 55 mph at the "Slow Down" ahead sign. Describe the safety level the lead car demonstrates when starting the slow-down process.

b) In the bottom part of the illustration, could or should Ashley have thought that the car ahead of her "brake checked her"?

a) If Ashley had been tailgating the car in front of her for a while, do you think that the car in front of her was safe (even though they were legal) in slowing down where they did when they saw the sign?

b) Suppose Ashley's car had better braking and acceleration than the car in front of her (maybe it was a performance vehicle). Was she justified in passing the car on the double yellow line if there was no oncoming traffic?

c) When the speed limit dropped to 25 mph about 400 feet after the slowdown sign, Ashley not only reduced her speed to the limit but also hit her brakes hard enough that the car behind her had to stop suddenly as well.
   a. Why do you think Ashley did this?
   b. How was the driver behind her likely to interpret this behavior?
   c. Ashley was braking to the speed limit or perhaps slightly below it. Is her behavior as shown here legal? Safe?

d) What are some reasons why areas reduce the speed limit to 25mph or lower? What are the dangers of ignoring these limits? What other types of road signs or conditions should you watch for when speed limits drop?

The Automobile Anger Apprentice

Ashford and Ashley rage as they ride.
Cursing! Honking! With anger and pride.
Ashwin starts to repeat...
Ashlyn hides in defeat...
Road rage habits are hard to subside.

Humans, for the most part, are sponges. They absorb a wide range of input and learn from the moment they are born. Many people believe driver education begins in the teenage years, but it actually starts at birth. Humans watch, listen to, and experience the actions and attitudes of parents, siblings, and other adults when they drive, even if the driver is in another car, in a movie, on TV, or on social media. Children inherit attitudes and habits from nearly everywhere.

Things to think about, write about, or discuss

a) Have you ever noticed your parents doing something they shouldn't while driving? This question is relevant for young drivers, parents, grandparents, and older users of these materials!

a) Describe what you think the baby in the car seat is learning.

b) Describe what you believe the tween in the back seat is learning.

c) What actions should you take as a driver next to, slightly behind, or passing this car full of Ashes?

d) Suppose you did something rude or wrong as a driver near the Ashes. We know their reaction isn't appropriate. What could or should you do now that you've made a mistake and they are furious?

e) Is there ever a point where you should or are even obligated to call 911 because of raging drivers with children in the car? Or is there never a situation where you should do this? Discuss the subtleties of this decision.

f) Describe a time when you were driving and got angry over something that, after a moment of reflection, you were embarrassed by. How could you have avoided reacting with anger? How can you become aware of your anger? What steps can you take to calm down?

Root cause: Learned Behaviors

You learn what you live.

Aggressive driving and road rage can be learned behaviors. That's why it's important to stay emotionally in control while driving around children of all ages.

Drivers are influenced by their parents, other adults, friends, and the norms they grow up with.

Young children, tweens, and even teenagers pick up actions and behaviors they've observed throughout their lives.

These behaviors are observed not only from parents, friends, and family. They can also be seen on the road, at home within viewing and listening distance of a road, and in movies, on television, and on social media.

If aggressive driving is considered normal or positive, people may adopt these behaviors as part of their driving style.

That's why it is key to minimize or stop aggressive behaviors in the car as soon as the baby is buckled into the car seat on the way home from the hospital.

The Dubious Donut Derby

Ashley floored it, her eyes on the glaze,
"Red lights? Speed limit? I'm on a craze.
What's this? The light is green?!
I need coffee and cream!
I am lost in a sugar-starved haze."

Sometimes, we all need to get somewhere quickly. The best approach is to plan enough time to drive there safely.

Ashes don't always behave that way. Sometimes, others just have to marvel at the risky, poor decisions that Ashes make and understand why they made them. And learn from them.

Things to think about, write about, or discuss

a) What dangerous thing or things did Ashley do?

b) Why does it seem she is doing them?

c) Ashley broke some laws. Isn't it ironic that others limited her progress in her "road race?" Who else is breaking the law, and why?

d) Realistically, how much time did Ashley save if her entire journey was 30 minutes?

e) Discuss the increased risks and dangers (driving, temper, legal issues, other factors) her actions created.

f) Are there any situations where a driver can or should pass on a double-yellow or speed to reach a destination? If so, what are they?

g) In certain emergencies of a specific intensity, what options should you consider to help you get somewhere quickly?

h) Explain why it might be justified to cut someone off and cross the double-yellow line. Is it worth it for Krispy Kreme Donuts? Voodoo Donuts? Dunkin' Donuts? Local places like Bob's? Now, describe what may happen if you decide to do so.

i) What could or should you do if you were a passenger in Ashley's car in this situation?

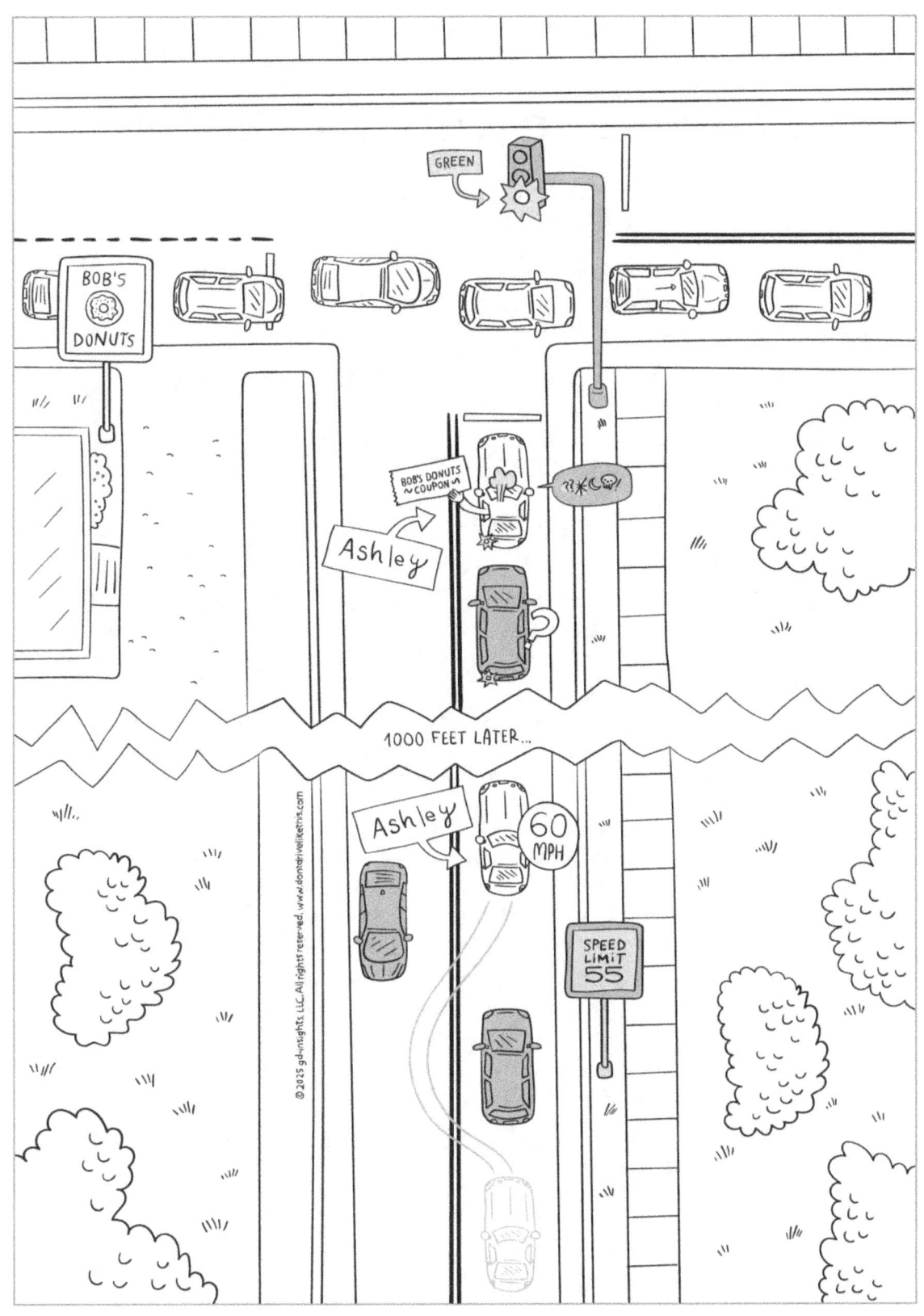

The Scared and the Sprayed

Ashford's truck, piled dangerously high,
Soil and stone in a heap to the sky.
Bits flew loose with a crack,
Windshields hit with a whack!
Passing for safety? Plans gone awry.

Owning a pick-up truck is essential for landscaping, moving items, and many other transport tasks. Whether you run a business or are a weekend warrior, you are responsible for properly securing all loads and covering loose material that could blow off onto the road or other vehicles.

Things to think about, write about, or discuss

a) What has Ashford done wrong?

b) Who is responsible for the crack in the windshield of the car behind Ashford? For the truck two slots behind Ashford, which is indirectly being hit by materials bouncing off the road or the car in front of it?

a) Ashley is in a challenging situation. She doesn't want to speed up and pass as she will enter the "spray" of materials from Ashford's truck. It is usually advisable not to ride beside a flatbed transport truck, even if the pipes or other materials appear secure.
   1. What can Ashley do now?
   1. If she decides that dropping back is the proper course of action, how can she effectively communicate her intentions? Indicator lights? Hand gestures? Brake taps? All? Other?
   2. What should the car behind Ashley do? What situational awareness and patience should that driver demonstrate?

b) What is the best way to indicate to Ashford that he needs to pull over and secure his load?

c) At what point, if any, should any of the vehicles in this illustration place a call to the police? If they do, should it be an emergency 911 call or a standard call to a local police department?

d) What actions, if any, and when, should vehicles on the other side of the divided highway take?

Avoidance Technique: Safely Exiting Situations

When confronted with aggressive or raging drivers:

Avoid engaging with them. Don't make eye contact or respond to provocations. Give as much physical space as possible on the road.

Removing yourself from the situation is typically the best and first option unless there is an obvious safety issue.

Avoidance doesn't make you a wimp. Imagine the possible outcomes if you or your passengers interact with an already angry and aggressive driver. "Flip the script" and view avoidance as a "win."

Safely change lanes or move to increase distance. Do not stop and leave the vehicle.

Don't try to de-escalate when a rager keeps raging after you offer a quick, visual "Sorry" gesture. More words and hand gestures might provoke even more self-righteous rage.

Don't take it personally. If you made a driving mistake, it wasn't you who then escalated the situation.

If you are threatened in a way that you cannot immediately avoid, find a safe public place with other people present to pull over and call for help. Ask a passenger to call or call yourself. Most states have an exception for using a handheld phone in urgent safety situations.

The Menacing Merging Misfit

Ashley barreled straight onto the road,
Ignoring proper yields from the code.
With some cars in her way,
She merged into the fray.
Now traffic is a panicked commode!

Ashley is indeed "entering" traffic from an onramp. But let's not call it merging, m'kay? It's more of a "I'm merging, get out of my way."

Things to think about, write about, or discuss

a) Why is Ashley merging this way?

b) Based on the traffic pattern in this picture, what should she have done instead?

c) Describe the rare situations when it would have been OK for Ashley to come to a full stop on an onramp. Or is it never appropriate or legal?

d) Who has the right of way in this situation?

e) What are some good practices if an onramp is unusually short?

f) What are good practices for Ashley if her vehicle isn't capable of accelerating quickly?

g) If Ashley's vehicle is more powerful than the cars near her already on the highway, what impact should that have on how she approaches merging into traffic from the onramp?

h) When, if ever, is a car already on the highway legally required to move over to give way to a car merging from an onramp?

i) When, if ever, is it a good idea to yield for etiquette reasons? Or not to yield for etiquette reasons?

j) How do Ashley's rear-view mirrors, her view (or lack thereof) through her back window, driving technology in her vehicle, and her ability to turn her head around to see current highway traffic potentially affect safety in this traffic situation?

The Besieged Bicyclists

At the lights, chaos reigns in the air.
Ashford curses! Gives cyclists a scare.
Ashley shouts at the lane,
Ashton's cycling's insane.
This shared road is chock full of despair.

Bicycles not only deserve to, but also have the legal right to share the road. This should be acknowledged by both motorists and cyclists.

Things to think about, write about, or discuss

a) Motorist Ashley is yelling at a cyclist to get on the sidewalk, while a pedestrian is yelling at Ashton the cyclist to get off the sidewalk.
   1. Which "screamer" is legally correct?
   2. Should the "screamer" who is correct have used a different method to communicate, or just have dropped it as they weren't going to change someone else's behavior?

b) What is Ashford doing, and besides his rage, is there anything else Ashford is doing that should be changed?

c) Is the cyclist next to Ashford doing anything wrong?

d) If you're a cyclist and know you're doing everything legally and correctly, but the traffic around you doesn't acknowledge your rights, what should you do to stay safe?

e) If you are a motorist who knows you're acting correctly and legally but the cyclists around you don't recognize your rights, what should you do to keep all parties safe?

f) In what situations can a cyclist hit a car with their hand or an object?

g) Is there ever a situation where a driver should take an aggressive action (like revving their engine, pretending to move over, or tossing a non-lethal object at the cyclist) to warn or get a cyclist's attention?

h) In your area, if you are a cyclist, are you legally permitted to wear headphones to listen to music, wear only one earbud, or not wear headphones at all? Regardless of local laws, what is the safest option and why?

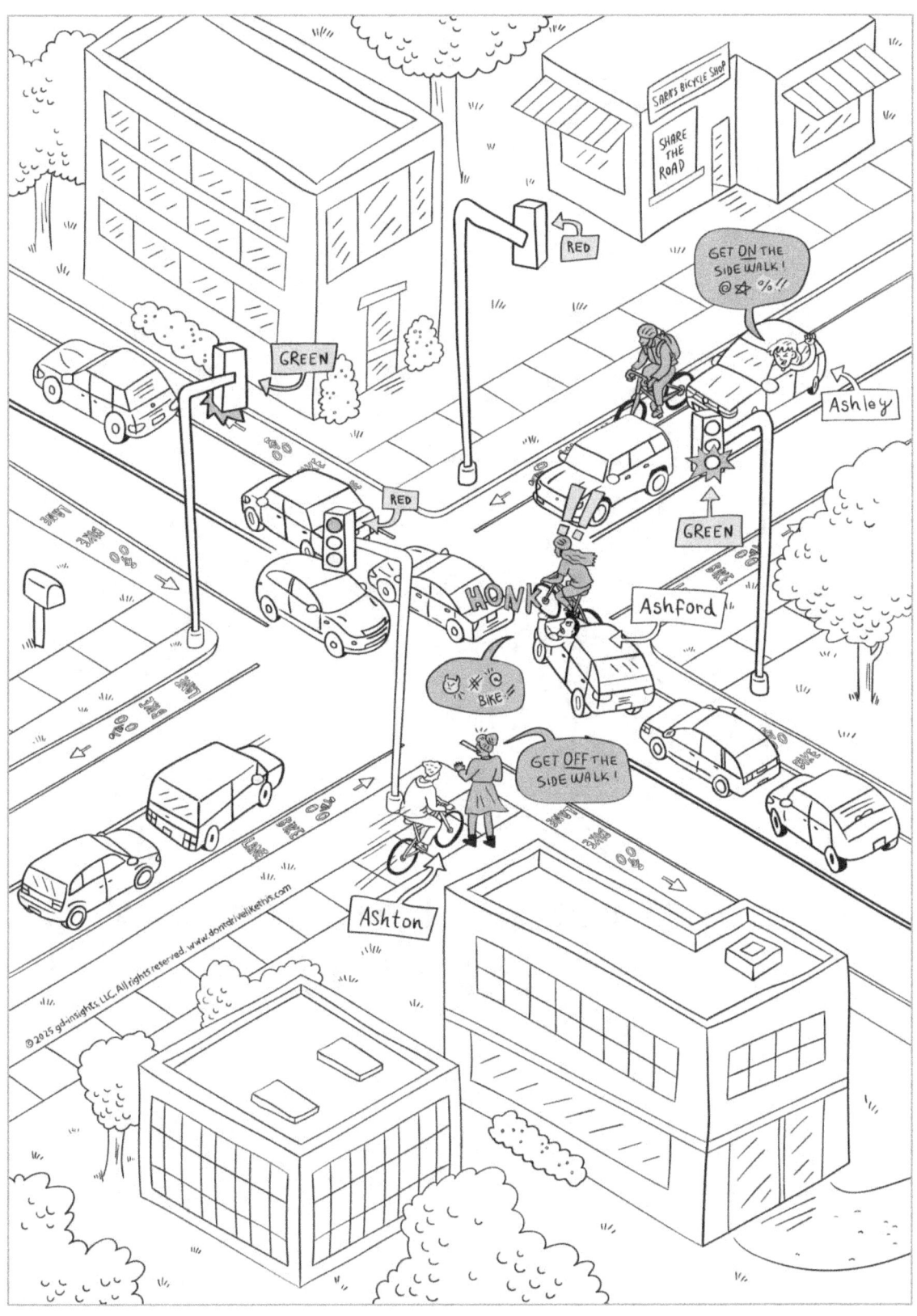

Root cause: Empathy (or Lack of It)

Aggressive drivers may struggle to show empathy toward others and to "put themselves in another's shoes."

They may not realize that other drivers could be dealing with emergencies or genuine mistakes and often assume the worst intentions of others. This can lead to anger instead of understanding.

Can you admit that you make mistakes sometimes too?

Perhaps the same mistake you're complaining or raging about?

Is an aggressive response to someone else's actions truly the best way to handle things on the road? In your life?

The Risk-Taking Roadway Reverser

Missing his exit, Ashford went back,
Quick reverse onto the white and black.
The car behind swerved wide,
Ash ignorant inside!
His dumb stunt nearly caused a car stack.

Sometimes you miss an exit. Sometimes the next turn around spot is far away. That's life. We all make navigation mistakes.

Things to think about, write about, or discuss

a) What reasons might Ashford have had for making this move, despite safety and legality concerns?

b) What could Ashford have planned better to avoid missing an exit?

c) How could Ashford have been driving on the highway that prevented him from reaching the exit on time or properly?

d) If someone else on the road prevented Ashford from taking this exit (either intentionally or by accident), does that affect his right to reverse back onto the exit ramp?

e) If Ashford insisted on executing this maneuver, what could he have done to make it somewhat safer? Why is this question inappropriate?

f) Whose responsibility would it be if any of the cars behind Ashford quickly maneuvered in a way that caused a collision?

g) What, if anything, could the authorities have done to address this illegal activity based on the current activities shown in this illustration?

h) Would the cars nearest to Ashford have been useful by honking in this situation? If so, how would honking have helped? If not, could honking have caused any harm?

i) What actions should the car at the start of the exit ramp take or refrain from based on Ashford's actions?

The Specs, Drugs, and Self Control

Three houses, three drivers, all with flaws:
Ashley's mad, she and Ash in a brawl.
Ashton's meds are severe,
Ashanti's eyes? Can she steer?
On this street, every driver is flawed.

Ah, mornings on the commute to school or work in areas where you have to drive and can't use public transportation! Things can happen before you get in the car that might have you driving like an Ash!

Things to think about, write about, or discuss

a) Describe the general concerns and conditions of each of the Ashes in Ash Acres who are preparing to drive during rush hour.

b) What options does Ashton have with his doctor, family, or employer to make his drive safer for himself and others?

c) Why could Ashton be pulled over and charged with impaired driving even if there's no alcohol detected on his breath or in his blood?

d) Ashanti forgot her glasses, which are required on her driver's license. What options does she have to prevent this from happening again?

e) In your jurisdiction, if Ashanti gets into a collision that isn't her fault, how might not wearing glasses affect fault? Could it influence insurance claims? Might she get a citation?

f) Ashford and Ashley are "at it" again. They're even arguing before Ashley gets in the car! How could this level of anger and conflict affect Ashley's driving?
    1. Her focus?
    2. Reaction time?
    3. Aggression?
    4. What could Ashley do to ease tension before or during the drive?

g) Is there more danger posed by the Ashes to the drivers in their neighborhood who are slowly entering highway traffic, or to the drivers on the rush-hour highway? How would a less congested time of day impact these dangers, if at all?

Avoidance Technique: Lifelong Learning

No matter your age or experience, continually improve your driving skills and knowledge.

Here are a few ideas:

Take additional defensive driving courses to boost your confidence and skills on the road.

Learn anger management techniques through books, workshops, or professional guidance in a way that aligns with your belief system.

Stay updated on the newest traffic laws and research-backed best practices for safe driving.

Read about the best way to use safety and automation design and technology for the vehicles you drive daily.

It's important to learn about vehicles with unfamiliar feaatures and technologies that are not present in your "daily driver." You never know when you may need to drive a rental car or a borrowed vehicle that has these technologies or features.

The Competitive, Confrontational Commuter

Raced to work with a wild, frantic grin,
Saved no time, then forgot to log in.
Cause his stress dragged him down,
On his calls, was a clown.
Missed a promotion he planned to win.

The bottom line of this illustration is math. Read the research reports. Use AI modeling. Even do your own back-of-the-napkin calculations. A typical aggressive, nonstop weaving commuter will save only a trivial amount of time on a crowded highway commute. Sure, sometimes they *might* gain a few minutes. But these drivers almost always slow down others, increase stress, and risk (or actually cause) collisions.

Things to think about, write about, or discuss

a) Discuss times someone has cut around you in traffic, only to see them at the traffic light miles ahead, arriving at almost the same time as you did.

b) Describe your feelings during a 20, 30, or 40-minute drive when you've been dangerously passed a dozen times, and you peel your fingers off the steering wheel when you get to work.

c) Would you consider leaving earlier to drive more relaxed?

d) Are deep breathing and thinking about relaxing while you drive techniques that can really slow you down and improve your mood and attitude, possibly for the entire day? Research, discuss, and propose alternatives.

e) What is the impact on auto wear and tear and fuel efficiency during weaving in stop-and-go traffic? For the weaving driver? And for you, as you respond to the situations they create?

f) What are some things you, as the driver, can do to keep your passengers relaxed in these situations? What should your response be when a passenger insists you weave or pass when you don't want to? How can you respond with good humor?

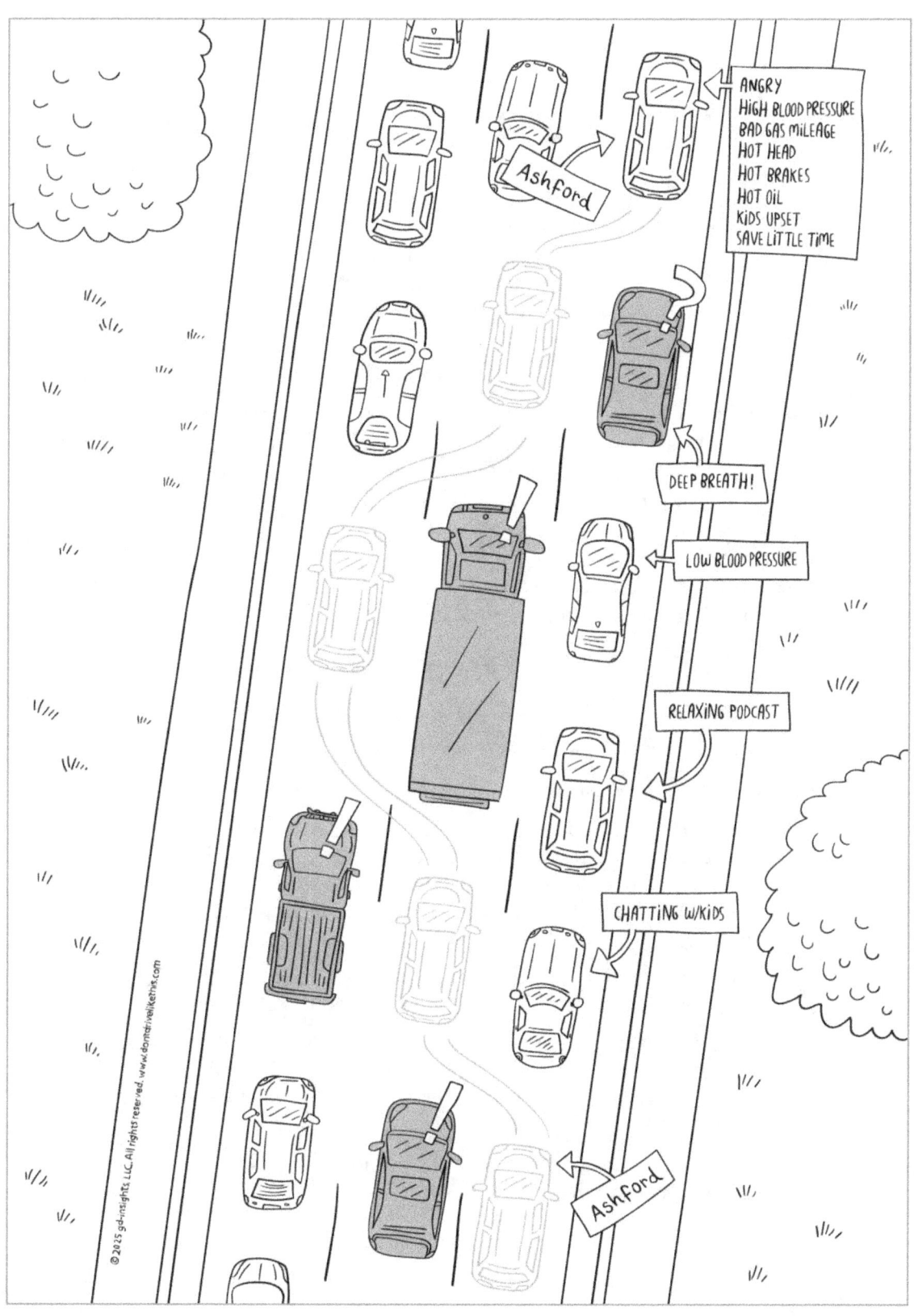

The Zip It, Don't Clip It!

Two lanes to one, where zippering's neat,
Take your turn! Please don't cheat.
Except Ash—a big jerk,
He'll squeeze, tailgate, and twerk.
Let us hope that their bumpers don't meet.

Courteous drivers entering Burgstown seem to be merging smoothly from a four-lane road onto a two-lane road in town. The through lane (the left lane in this case) has the right of way. When traffic is heavy (shown here), the "zipper" method is recommended—use both lanes fully until reaching the merge point, then cars closest to the merge take turns merging alternately. This helps keep traffic moving.

When traffic is lighter (not shown) and traffic is moving close to the speed limit, merging earlier can be a good choice.

Things to think about, write about, or discuss

a) Ashford is *trying* to zipper. What is he doing wrong?

b) What should Ashford have done instead?

c) What safe and legal options does the car to the left of Ashford have?

d) In slow, crowded conditions where zippering is correct and encouraged, what should a person who is properly trying to zipper do if someone in the through lane isn't letting them in when it's their turn, they are driving at a safe speed, and they are correctly signaling?

e) If the merge is happening in a construction zone, are there other things you need to consider for a lane merging situation?

f) Is zipper merging generally considered more efficient in slow-moving traffic merge situations? What positive or negative effects does zipper merging have on speed, efficiency, and road rage when executed correctly or poorly?

g) What other common mistakes or unkind actions do Ashes often make during merge situations?

Root cause: Anonymity

When you dance, dance as if nobody is watching.

When you drive, drive as if everybody is watching.

Strangely, some consider their behavior inappropriate and dangerous only when they are identifiable.

If you get aggressive while driving, do you ever feel embarrassed or less angry if you realize someone nearby sees you losing your temper? Or if you recognize the person watching you?

The anonymity of driving can increase road rage.

People tend to behave better when they know someone is watching. The lessons from psychology experiments, where children act differently when they know others are watching, are relevant here.

People sometimes believe it's okay to be aggressive because they won't see the other driver again. This makes them feel less responsible for their actions.

The Wild West Weapon Wielder

Ashford stormed out, a bat in his hand,
Night's silence was tense. It wasn't planned.
The target backed away.
The gas clerk screamed out "Hey!"
Ash's rage is a part of his brand.

This is one of the ugliest situations that out-of-control road rage can cause in our communities. There is never a reason to get out of your car with a weapon or to use one while in a vehicle, no matter what someone else does. There is always a way to step away, and you're not wimpy for doing so. Let's flip the script!

Things to think about, write about, or discuss

a) Why might Ashford believe he has the right to stop his car, get out, and brandish a baseball bat?

b) Could the car behind Ashford have done anything to justify Ashford's actions?

c) Is the driver behind Ashford taking the correct actions?

d) In most jurisdictions, is the driver behind Ashford allowed to use a mobile phone while driving in this situation? Even if not, is it the right thing to do in this case?

e) Is the person at the gas station handling the situation correctly? Should they physically intervene, retreat into the store and lock the door, or take another action?

f) If the driver behind Ashford knows the area, where should they go? If they don't know the area, where should they go?

g) If you are Ashford, or even somewhat an Ashford, what could you have done differently, regardless of the danger, idiocy, or perceived slight you experienced from the car behind you?

h) Perform an internet search on "criminal road rage," "vehicular assault," or "violent road rage," and consider the injury and chaos resulting from these incidents. Discuss how all parties could have managed these situations more effectively.

The Kill 'Em with Kindness

The left turn is our Ashley's intent.
An attempt at true kindness she meant.
All her waving ignored,
The cars behind her soared!
Ash's kindness could get some cars bent

Ashley thinks she's being kind by waving a car on the side road to turn ahead of her onto the main road. Unfortunately, the car on the side road isn't turning, and Ashley is getting frustrated. Vehicles behind her are beginning to pass her on the shoulder to her right.

Things to think about, write about, or discuss

a) Which vehicle turning has the right of way, and why?

b) What are the legal and safety concerns for the cars behind Ashley that are passing her on the right using the shoulder?

c) Why are or why aren't Ashley's actions truly "kind"?

d) Does Ashley waving at a car create any legal exception to violations that might be happening around her because of her action, which is a clear gesture for someone else to turn in front of her?

e) Once the line of cars behind Ashley begins to pass her on the right, what is the best action for the vehicle signaling to turn onto Main Street?

f) At this moment, which vehicles could get a citation in most jurisdictions, and why?

g) Let's suppose:
   1. The second car behind Ashley in this illustration then stops behind Ashley, whose turn signal is still on and is waving. The second car follows the law and *doesn't* pass on the right shoulder.
   2. This car, now directly behind Ashley, intends to continue to drive up Main Street and is *not* indicating a left turn.
   3. When Ashley eventually makes her left turn, what dangers are present with (i) the cars that decided to stop behind Ashley, (ii) the cars passing on the shoulder, and (iii) the car on the side street trying to turn left onto Main Street?

h) Is there ever a situation, under these conditions, where it is safer to break the law than to follow it exactly?

Avoidance Technique: Mindset and Perspective - I

Cultivate a positive mindset while driving.

Practice gratitude by focusing on the positives, such as the ability to travel and see new, scenic views.

Perhaps you have a good job and coworkers or great teachers and friends that you'll see at the end of your drive.

Focus on something positive rather than fixating on traffic or the poor behavior of others.

And remember that everyone makes mistakes. Other drivers? Sure, they do. But you make mistakes as well.

Handle tough driving situations with empathy and poise.

Avoid taking other drivers' actions personally or letting them make you angry.

The Rogue Road Racers

Team Ash, weaving through cars causing screams,
Treating the highway like wild daydreams.
Twice the limit they race,
A death trap in each case!
Straight to jail or the grave is the theme.

Motorcycles have every right to be on the road. And 99.5% of them are responsible and respectful, and probably more in danger from auto drivers than auto drivers are of them. That said, there is always the exception of illegal street racing. This puts everyone in danger.

Things to think about, write about, or discuss

a) You may feel scared or angry if a Team Ashford and Team Ashley weave around you in a street race. What are things you should avoid doing to increase the chances of staying safe?

b) What are the key principles of defensive driving that are essential to help you stay safe around reckless speeders going 30 mph or more above the speed limit?

c) What steps should you take to increase the chances of a safe outcome for you and your passengers?

d) If the prevailing traffic is 65 mph and a street race occurs with speeds twice the limit, what is the safest action: speed up as fast as you can, slow down, maintain your current speed, or something else? How would your reactions differ if the race is with cars or motorcycles?

e) Which lane should you stay in or switch to if Team Ashford or Team Ashley approaches you from behind at lightning speeds?

f) If you ride a motorcycle, what are some ways to avoid getting involved in an illegal street race?

g) What is it like to 'stay calm' around a dozen loud, fast illegal street racers who might be trying to intimidate you and others?

h) If you purposely cause a collision with an Ash who is a reckless, aggressive speeder, whose fault is the collision? What are the implications at that moment, and for your future should you choose to "aggress on the aggressor?"

The Furtive Funeral Finagler

In town, the procession was somber.
Ashley's kindness? 'Twas hers to squander.
She stepped on it; Right through!
Screw the funeral queue.
Respect for the grieving? Let's ponder.

Funerals are occasions when showing respect and politeness is essential. Most places have specific laws, and everyone has informal etiquette that you should learn and follow to demonstrate respect.

Study and discuss the laws in your jurisdiction and etiquette with your instructor and peers. While funerals are not as common as other road situations, it's important to know how to behave. Consider how you would feel if the procession were for someone you loved.

Things to think about, write about, or discuss

a) What actions is Ashley taking that she shouldn't be? What should she have done instead?

b) There is one car turning in this illustration that is not part of the funeral procession. Why is or isn't this okay?

c) What did Ashley miss or ignore in the line of cars in the center? Is the procession properly marked?

d) If the procession is on a multi-lane highway and it is in a single lane, per law and etiquette, could Ashley pass it?
   1. On the left, if the procession is traveling in the right lane?
   2. On the right, if the procession is traveling in the left lane?

e) What should you do when your car is near a funeral procession, whether your vehicle is moving or not?

f) When police are present in vehicles or on the street helping to direct a funeral procession, what should you do and what should you not do?

g) Discuss how you would feel if you were in a funeral procession mourning a lost loved one and a nearby car played loud music obliviously and cut into or through the procession.

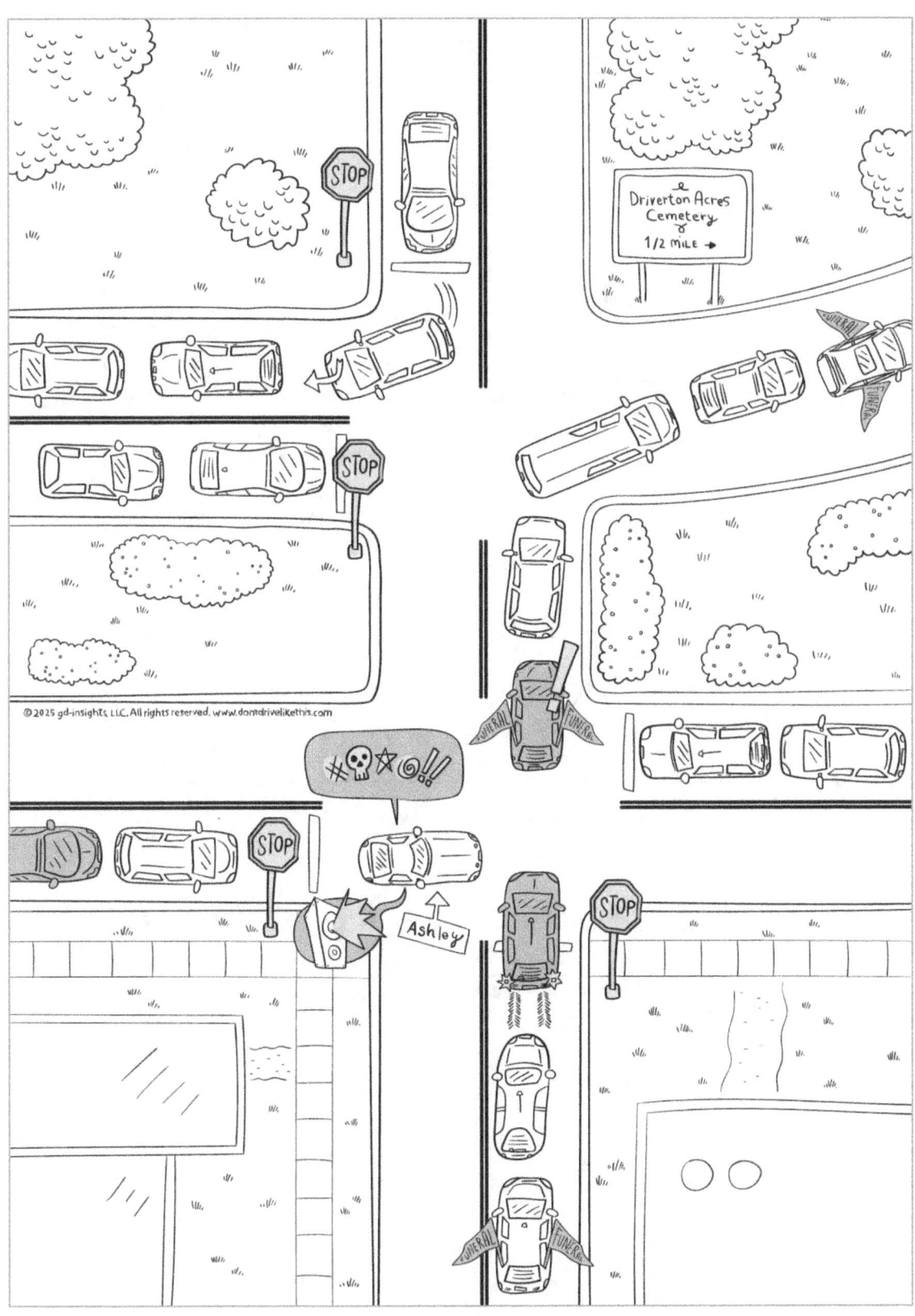

Root cause: "Taking It Out" on Other Drivers

Some people can't always (or ever!) handle stress and anger in a healthy way. Everyone experiences moments like this. Some of us go through many of them.

Suppose you get a bad grade, get laid off, or your girlfriend, boyfriend, or spouse is angry with you. Or your furnace breaks down and you have to take out a loan to fix it. Or you didn't make the team. Or any one of a million other things that life throws at you.

People handle situations like this by taking a long walk or run, meditating, talking on the phone with friends, speaking to a therapist, playing video games, praying, or venting on social media. These activities, among others, may or may not help you, but they probably won't cause harm or kill anyone.

If you want to express your anger and frustration from other areas of your life by jumping in a vehicle and speeding, doing donuts, throwing things out the window, or saying "I am going to teach this idiot a lesson" to another driver, you need to explore avoidance techniques.

Road rage is contagious, and you'll give it to others as a present! According to the American Psychological Association, 50% of drivers respond to careless acts of other drivers with aggressive behavior themselves.

Negative, aggressive actions won't make you feel better in the long term, no matter what you think.

The Left Turn Laceration

In his car, Ashford felt quite supreme.
Turning left was a selfish daydream.
From the right Ashford veered,
Left-turners they all feared,
That he'd cause a big car crashing meme.

Ashford is clearly making multiple unsafe assumptions and taking risky actions.

Things to think about, write about, or discuss

a) What are the legal and practical options for the car that Ashford is cutting off to make a left turn?

b) What could Ashford have done instead of attempting to make a left turn from a right-turn-only lane?

c) What kind of danger is each of these cars in?
   1. Ashford.
   2. The car he is cutting off.
   3. The car safely stopped at the light (on the top left), waiting for the traffic signal to change.
   4. The second car, behind the car being cut off, that is moving slowly to make a left turn in the left turn lane.

d) Do you think this situation would have improved with additional signage? What action would Ashford likely have taken with more signage beyond the painted lines and traffic signal arrow?

e) If pedestrians were on specific sidewalks visible in this illustration, describe what danger they might be in if this situation resulted in a collision.

f) If pedestrians attempt to cross at this intersection, which lacks crosswalks or pedestrian signs, explain who would and wouldn't be responsible if a vehicle hits a pedestrian, and why?

g) While annoying, if Ashford is doing something he could get a citation for, what would it be? If there were a collision between him and the car behind him, who would be responsible?

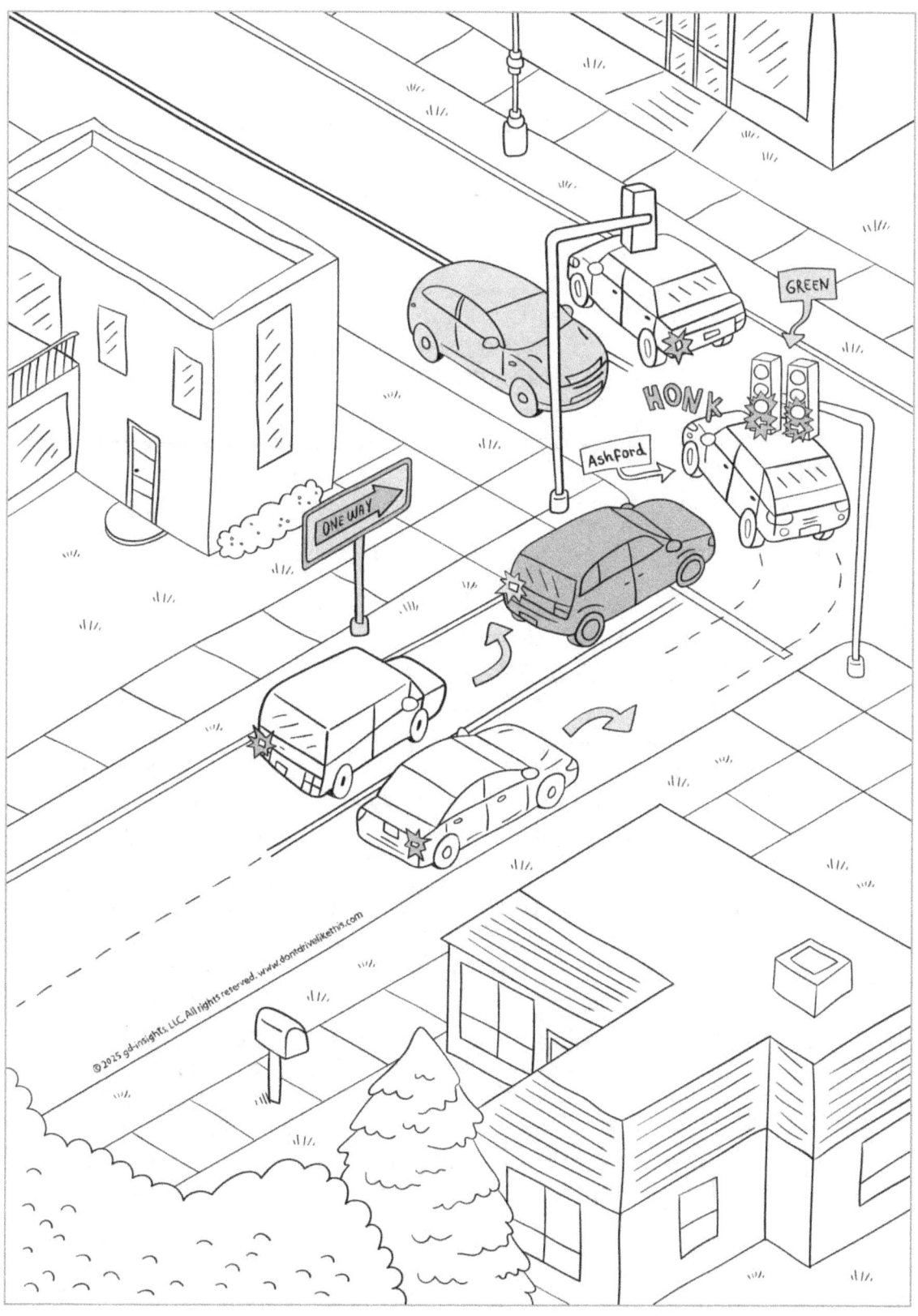

The Stressed-Out Student Driver

In the school zone, the honking won't cease.
Ashley and Ashford both smash the peace.
Student driver up front,
Carries most of the brunt.
And the teachers just hope for release.

Student drivers face many challenges. This student driver is going below the speed limit and looks unsure. Plus, school zones can be hectic! Shouldn't everyone remember what it was like to learn how to drive?

Things to think about, write about, or discuss

a) What things is Ashley doing wrong or rudely?

b) Who do you think the car behind the student driver is frustrated with?

c) Why do you think Ashford is honking, and is his honking justified?

d) Discuss the factors in this situation that might be causing stress for the student driver. Consider the positions and speeds of cars, driver actions, lights, pedestrian locations, and environmental sounds.

e) How might this situation change if the School Zone sign wasn't flashing?

f) What are some ways the student driver could have prepared for the sensory environment they are experiencing?

g) What are some ways the student driver can help reduce their sensory overload in the moment?

h) Which cars in this illustration are engaged in actions that might be considered poor etiquette or could result in a citation in most jurisdictions if a police officer strictly followed the regulations of an active school zone?

i) Some drivers in this illustration seem to be turning or preparing to turn. In what situations is it legal for drivers to opt not to use their turn signals because limited turn options show which way they will most likely turn?

Avoidance Technique: Emotional Awareness

People experience awareness and control of their emotions in different ways. Try to recognize, understand, and manage your feelings while you're driving.

This isn't an easy task, regardless of your age. Consider how you feel about emotions and driving, from observing others to your own experiences behind the wheel. Think about your emotional awareness in other parts of your life.

For example:
- Recognize your personal early warning signs of anger or frustration.
- Reframe your negative thoughts about other drivers. Think of different reasons for their mistakes or actions that help you be more understanding and less angry.
- Focus on your actions and what you can control instead of worrying about things outside your influence.

It is important to think about, read about, and discuss these things with peers, advisors, parents, and instructors.

Whether you are young or old, a new driver or an experienced one, there are always more things to learn about your emotions, how to manage them, and how they influence your reactions while driving.

The Four-Way Stop Situation

First car proceeds, now turners must choose.
But loud honking just made them confused.
Ashley's rage knew no end,
Ashford's voice did ascend.
Right-of-way rule books should be perused!

At a four-way stop, Car A has entered the intersection. Car B is signaling a turn, and Car C is also signaling a turn. Assume they arrived at the same time, and Car A was already well into the intersection.

Things to think about, write about, or discuss

a) According to the accepted rules and regulations for this situation, should Car B or Car C go next, and why?

In other situations, many variables must be considered. Which car arrived first? Turning directions? Which is the main road, and which is the side road? And more! Review your driver manual, other materials, and consult with instructors. For now, let's focus on the Ashes!

b) If Car B and Car C correctly determine who proceeds next, but the Ashes don't know or care about the rules, B and C should:
   1. Follow the rules both of them know, and ignore the Ashes.
   2. As a courtesy, use hand gestures to show who proceeds next.
   3. Get out of their cars and dump coffee on the Ash's cars.

c) Suppose this situation changes so that Car A, despite having the right of way for arriving first, waits for others proceed. This could confuse drivers. What communication techniques should B and C use to clarify who proceeds next when A ignores their right of way?

d) How are the Ashes affecting the confusion and safety at this intersection?

e) How does their noise and anger affect an already stressful situation, if in a driving situation, it's clear that not everyone knows the rules?

f) How should pedestrians at this four-way stop, especially without painted crosswalks, influence each of the drivers shown?

The Abrasive Accessibility Abuser

Accessible spots are marked with care.
Van ramps need eight to ten feet of air.
But our Ashford's quite dense,
Shows little common sense.
"A brief stop!" he aggressed unaware.

Ashford has broken some laws and been rude. For example, his truck is partially parked on the hash marks reserved for the unobstructed entrance and exit of people using an accessible van.

Things to think about, write about, or discuss

a) Is the spot where Ashford is parked, ignoring that he's on the hash marks, an accessible parking spot? Why or why not?

b) Identify current safety concerns experienced by the person using a wheelchair and the person assisting them.

c) Ashford only went into the store for a minute, and the people using the van weren't in it when he went in. How do you think he justified how and where he parked?

d) To enter the parking lot, the person using the wheelchair had to use a curb cut that was not the closest to the entrance of their van . Should they, and the person assisting, have waited on the sidewalk for safety reasons, regardless of Ashford's rudeness and rule-breaking?

e) Are all accessible parking spots "Van Accessible" parking spots?

f) What is the fine for parking in an accessible spot or blocking a van access point in your area? Is there a minimum amount of time you can block an accessible spot before a citation (ticket) can be issued?

g) What are the ways that a vehicle can be marked as legally permitted to use an accessible parking spot?

h) Given Ashford's exclamation, what should the person in the wheelchair and the person assisting say or do?

i) Is a passenger vehicle that is not a van, but has proper markings for an accessible spot, allowed to park in a van-accessible spot? Why or why not?

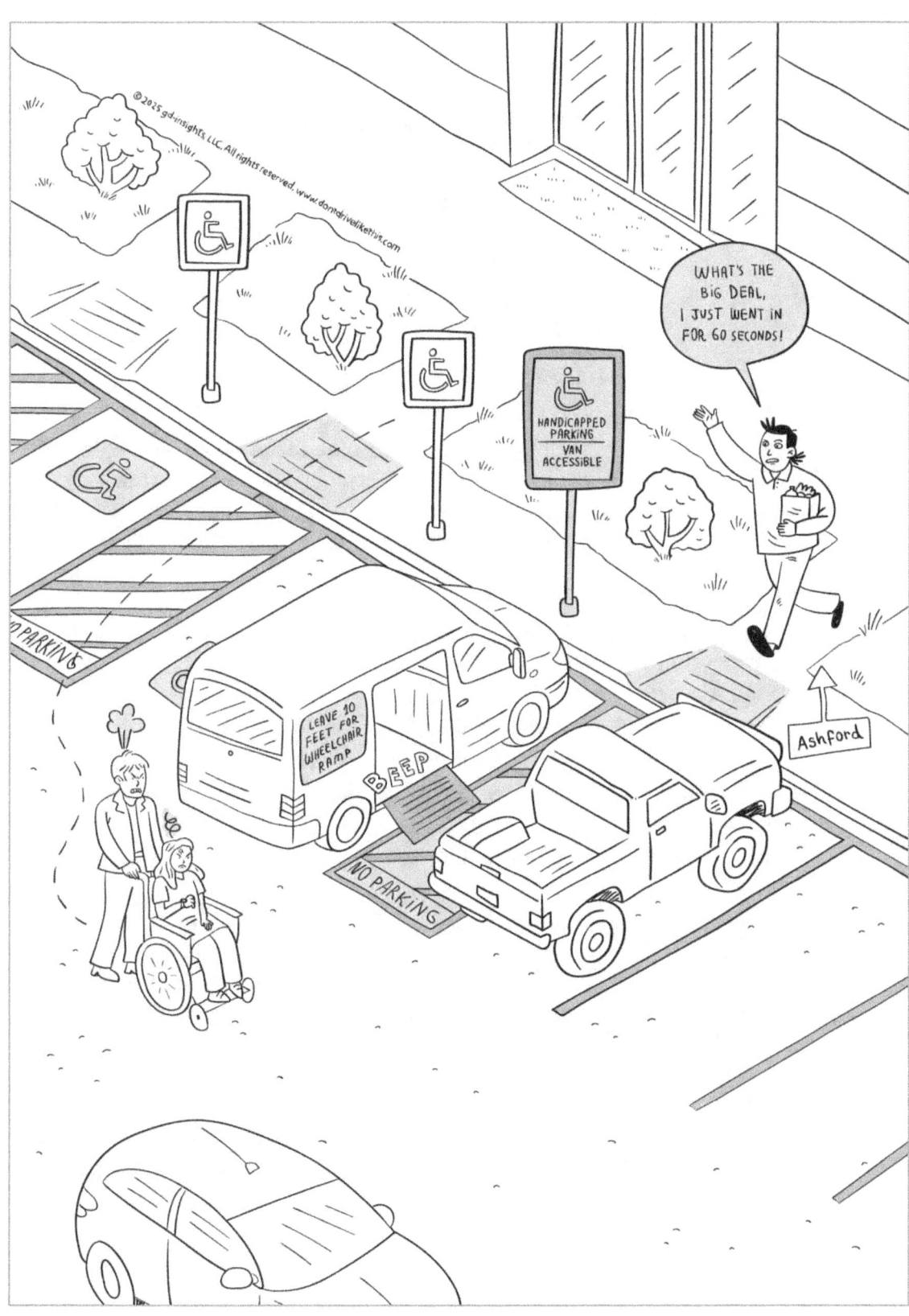

The Parking Lot Pull Through

Ashley thought she was queen of the lot,
Skipped three open spaces for her spot.
At a pull-through she whipped,
Car across nearly clipped
Now she's cursing, "You move I am not!"

Ashley is driving slowly, safely, and legally in the Mega Mart parking lot. Is she correct that "bay" or "nose-in" parking spots always allow the vehicle's front end to face forward because of a pull-through or back-in? Does that make for easier or safer exits? If so, does it apply to all vehicles?

Things to think about, write about, or discuss

a) What is happening in this illustration? Why did Ashley skip the four spots that were available?

b) Was Ashley correct in seeing a "pull through" spot and attempting to park by driving her truck through? What are your jurisdiction's rules regarding pull-through and back-in parking?

c) How can signage in a public or private lot affect pull-through and back-in parking?

d) Which lots in your area prohibit back-in and pull-through parking?

e) Pull-through or back-in parking, when permitted, can improve the visibility of pedestrians and vehicles, but also comes with risks and challenges depending on the vehicle, the lot, and the trip's purpose. Reflect on and explain how the benefits and risks of pull-through and back-in parking vary when a lot is jam-packed with people and cars compared to when it is mostly empty.

f) Does Ashley starting to move into the opposite spot affect the proper outcome of this story? Hint: Rules don't usually cover this, but does etiquette suggest Ashley should back up, park head-in, and call it a day? What other options are available? Is aggression or rage ever justified? How could either party step down from aggression should it occur?

Root cause: We're Animals. Well, We Are!

We must train ourselves to respond in more evolved, safer, and thoughtful ways. Especially when we face situations caused by someone driving like an Ash.

We are humans, and humans are animals. The fight-or-flight response to threats or perceived threats can turn small annoyances or big mistakes by others into anger.

"Quick to act without thought" responses are driven by the most primitive parts of our brains, responsible for automatic reactions. This is commonly called the "lizard brain."

Let's be clear: automatic responses, such as hitting the brakes to avoid a collision or turning sharply to dodge a child who runs into the street, are essential. We should be thankful that, with training, our nervous systems and brains can make certain driving actions almost automatic.

But there are driving decisions we should take a beat to process. Essentially, we must train our brains to pause our fight or flight instinct in the right situations. Usually, these involve emotional and impulsive reactions to an Ashley or Ashford. And in making sure we don't behave or drive like an Ash ourselves.

Despite our instinctual reactions, as humans, we have the capability to learn how to prevent our primal nature and threat response from controlling us. As drivers, we need to teach ourselves to make rational and safe decisions.

The Left Lane Exit Escalation

On the freeway, the left lane grew tight,
Left exit ahead plainly in sight.
Ashford raged at the slow,
Though the signs said to go.
He tailgated, sure he was right

Often, major multi-lane highways have some exits on the left side. These situations are clearly marked well in advance and again at the exit.

Things to think about, write about, or discuss

a) Based on what you observe or infer from this illustration, is the driver in front of Ashford doing everything possible to take Exit 21 safely?

b) How should the car in front of Ashford behave?
   1. Drive over the speed limit in passing lane traffic, then quickly slow down at the exit.
   2. Enter the fast lane and drive the speed limit or slower at least ½ mile in advance.
   3. Remain in the middle lane and cut across two lanes to exit left.
   4. Some other way, and if so, what way.

c) In your jurisdiction, what is the recommended distance for the vehicle in front of Ashford to signal their intention to exit left?

d) Let's assume the car in front of Ashford is behaving properly to exit.
   1. What thing or things is Ashford doing incorrectly?
   2. Who is Ashford endangering?
   3. Is the car in front of Ashford obligated to speed up?
   4. Is the car to the right of Ashford obligated to move over so Ashford can pass on the right?

e) What can we infer about Ashford's awareness of the situation and his knowledge of traffic rules?

f) When should the car in front of Ashford start to slow down?

g) What road conditions, weather conditions, signage, construction status, or other indicators demand that all parties consider more conservative decisions?

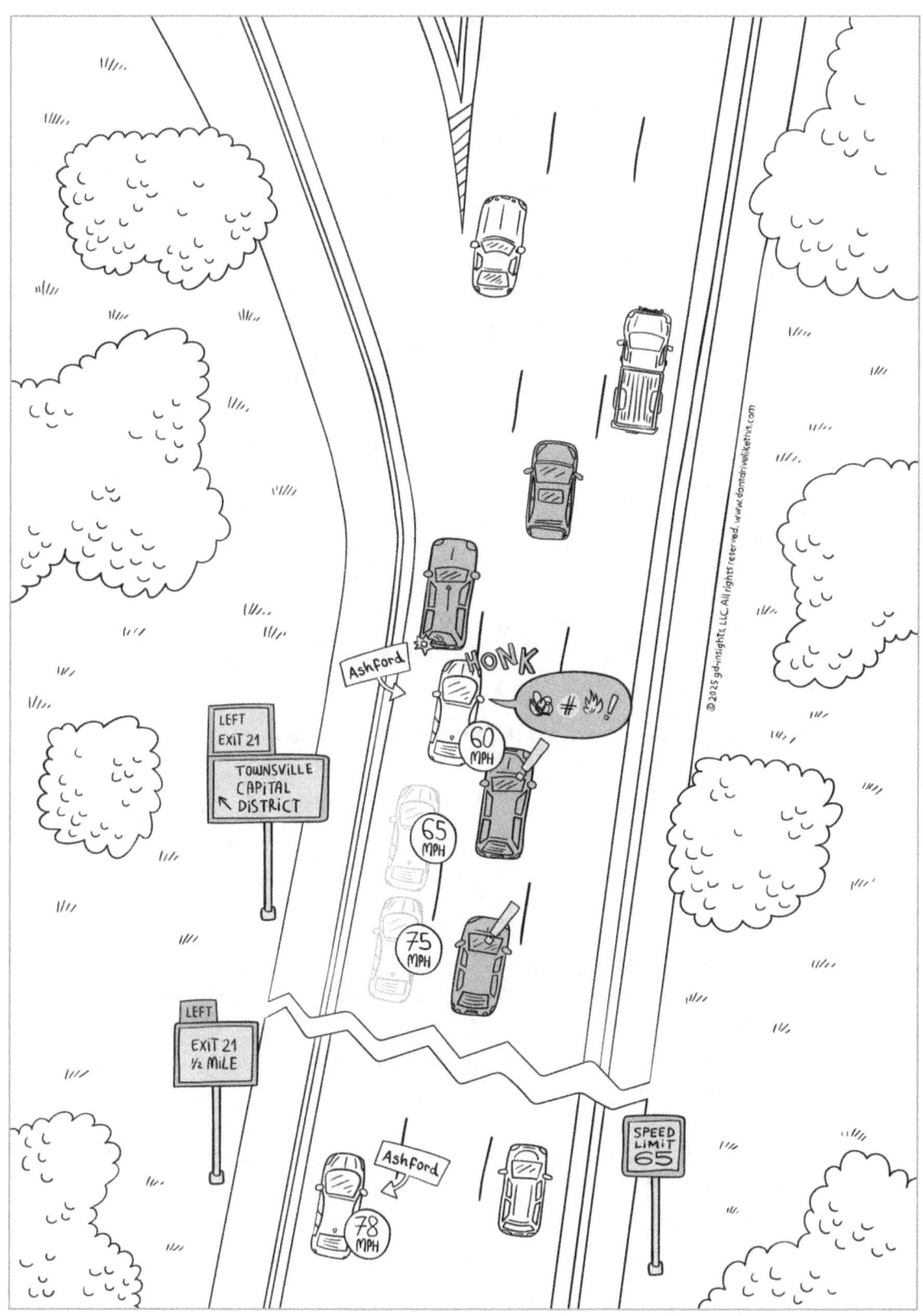

The Reckless Rescue Rubbernecker

Medics, cops, and tow trucks on the ground,
All moved over, save Ashley, the hound!
Her friend filmed for Insta,
Their souls, not a glimpse 'a,
Lack of feelings and safety abound.

Secondary collisions, which occur when drivers fail to move over or slow down near existing crashes or other road incidents involving emergency personnel, are a serious concern. According to various sources, not moving over during crashes results in dozens of deaths and many more injuries to emergency workers and other drivers.

Most don't "rubberneck," they are simply slowing down for safety. Slowing for safety is appropriate! But don't act like an Ash around active collision sites.

Things to think about, write about, or discuss

a) What signals, besides heavy traffic that is slowing down, can you notice to identify a collision or other event ahead to watch out for?

b) Suppose an Ash driving behind you doesn't see an emergency vehicle coming in their rear-view mirror, but you do. You slow down and move over, yet they seem like they're passing you as you pull over. What should you do?

c) In this illustration, Ashley is taking advantage of the extra safety space created by other cars properly slowing down and moving over. What offenses can Ashley likely be cited for in most jurisdictions?

d) Describe what might happen at this site because Ashley decided to drive like this.

e) Is there anything the other drivers, who are properly slowing down and moving over to the far left lane and shoulder, could or should do because of Ashley's decision to drive as she is?

f) What's the deal with Ashley's passenger?

Avoidance Technique: Ain't Nothing Like Courtesy

You're not responsible for other people's aggression. That said, since we live in the real world, driving safely and with courtesy not only prevents collisions, it lowers the chances of provoking road rage in others.

Remember, if someone else gets aggressive and rages, that is on them, even if you make a mistake. That's beyond your control. Simply apologize with a gesture and a mouthed "sorry," then move on safely. Rest assured, in their lives, they have also made errors in their driving.

The fundamentals are essential.

Always use your turn signals when changing lanes or making a turn.

Keep a safe distance from other vehicles. Don't tailgate.

Avoid weaving through traffic or making abrupt lane changes.

Use your horn sparingly and only as a safety warning, keeping it as short as possible for the situation.

Avoid using your horn to express anger or frustration. If you find yourself slamming your hand on the horn, you should try some relaxation techniques.

Follow local traffic laws and maintain a steady, safe speed, adjusting your speed to the road conditions.

The Literally Nobody Behind Me Turn

Ash's turn was self-centered danger,
Right of way? She's just a speed ranger.
The opposing car slammed,
Tires smoked and brakes jammed!
Selfish Ash just missed a life changer.

This illustration could depict a quiet town, a city at night, or a moment of lull in traffic. Regardless, Ashley causes some challenges.

Things to think about, write about, or discuss

a) Who has the right of way? Ashley, the car across from Ashley, or the car at the stop sign? Why?

b) What might be some reasons Ashley is turning in front of the other car? (Don't justify whether she is right or wrong, but what could be going on in her mind, and what is she focusing on?)

c) How can you avoid thinking or focusing differently than Ashley in ways that could lead to a better outcome?

d) If you are driving the car across from Ashley, what defensive actions could or should you have taken before this situation happened, and in the split second when it's happening?

e) If you're the person in the car stopped at the stop sign, what could or should you be doing right now? Anything different?

f) How would different weather conditions and times of day affect this situation?

g) If Ashley and the car in front of her collided, who would most likely be at fault for the crash?

h) We don't know the speed of either car in this illustration. Would the speed of Ashley and/or the car across from her affect the situation or determine who is at fault for a collision?

i) There are no pedestrians in this illustration. If there were pedestrians, what should drivers and pedestrians focus on in areas and situations like this?

The D³: The Distracted, Dangerous, Driver

One hand on her drink, the other on chat,
Eyes to her map; Eyes to this, then to that.
Quickly weaves across lanes
Sowing chaos and pain.
Ashley's distracted, let's pray there's no "Splat!"

Ashley considers many things essential to accomplish while driving. It's her moving couch. But doing multiple things at home on the couch presents a different, much lower risk to herself and others. It's a car, not a couch! You need a license to operate only one of them.

Things to think about, write about, or discuss

a) What physical activities is Ashley doing that distract her from properly controlling the car?

b) What effects do these activities have on her ability to focus on driving techniques that involve physical movement? For instance, effectively controlling the steering wheel or safely adjusting her body position if a beverage spills on her.

c) The same question as b), but apply it to mental focus, emotional focus, and proper visual scanning of her environment.

d) Should the cars around Ashley honk at her? If not, why not? If so, what duration of honk might effectively shift Ashley's focus?

e) Suppose the car to the right of Ashley was going slightly faster, and there was a collision when Ashley swerved into the right lane. Who would be responsible for the crash?

f) What are the recommended defensive driving moves for the car in front of Ashley, the car next to her, and the car behind her? What can the drivers around Ashley do to improve their own safety in this situation?

g) Is Ashley's activity and behavior in her car enough for any of the other cars in the illustration to call 911?

h) If you were a passenger in Ashley's car right now, what could or should you do to influence her behavior?

The Parallel Parking Putz

The parker shifted into reverse,
Behind, Ashley screamed loudly and cursed.
Ashford flew quickly by,
In the wrong lane—oh my!
Their rage spiraling forth in a burst.

Ashley and Ashford are both engaging in risky and aggressive driving. Ashley didn't stop early enough to allow the parallel parker to park. Ashford swerved into oncoming traffic to pass Ashley and the parker.

Things to think about, write about, or discuss

a) How could Ashley have avoided this whole situation?

b) Now that Ashford has (unsafely and illegally) opened up space behind Ashley, should Ashley reverse her car a bit and give the parker space to parallel park, or should the parker seek another spot?

c) Could and should Ashley get a citation for honking? Why or why not?

d) The two pedestrians shown in this illustration are on the sidewalk. Could this situation escalate into a danger for them?

e) Suppose the story here was that the parker tried to parallel park once already and failed to negotiate the spot. They are now on their second attempt to parallel park in that spot.
   1. Does this change anything? Are Ashley's frustration and action justified because she can park faster than this parker?
   2. Is it improper or illegal to attempt parallel parking a second time if you misjudge the first time? Why or why not?

f) If the oncoming car in the upper right driving toward Ashford was exceeding the speed limit and there was a collision, would the fault lie with Ashford, the oncoming car, or both parties?

g) Would any of the legal or safety considerations of the drivers' actions in this illustration change if the parallel parker was a student driver in a marked student driver vehicle? If so, how?

Root cause: Less Than Optimal Physical or Mental Health

Should mild or even severe health challenges prevent someone from driving safely? Not always, if the challenges are appropriately managed. Drivers and their family and social circles must stay aware of any issues and help ensure those challenges are handled. This is essential for the safety of the driver, passengers, and the public.

Physical health can influence aggressive driving. Challenges such as (but not limited to) chronic pain, sleep apnea, and insomnia may increase stress, impair clear thinking, and make people irritable and quick-tempered. This can lead to risky and aggressive driving. You can address these with help.

Underlying mental health conditions can sometimes exacerbate aggressive driving. People with depression, anxiety, post-traumatic stress disorder (PTSD), and other mental health challenges may struggle to control their emotions while driving. You can address these with help.

Aside from the risks of impaired driving, certain legal prescription drugs, some over-the-counter medications, and alcohol and cannabis—even when not currently in the driver's system—can increase aggressive driving.

Physical and mental health challenges don't automatically prevent someone from driving safely. Working with licensed mental and physical health practitioners is an excellent approach for many individuals and is an individual and family choice.

Please read the disclaimer on the copyright page.

The Impaired Imbiber, Inhaler, or Injector

Ash, impaired, takes his car for a spin.
Beer and pot both in sight, what a sin!
His road weavings a sight,
The mom's anger ignites.
Call the cops on this reckless has been!

This illustration depicts an exaggerated version of an impaired driver. Or does it? Is it truly exaggerated?

Things to think about, write about, or discuss

a) In what situations can a driver be pulled over for potential impairment, even if alcohol isn't immediately visible as shown in this illustration?

b) If Ashford had taken cannabis gummies or smoked pot before getting into the car, and he said he "felt OK," what would you advise him about driving?

c) How can a driver be considered impaired even if they haven't been drinking alcohol or using cannabis in any form?

d) Drivers using legally prescribed medications can still be charged with impaired driving. Why is this? How could this occur?

e) What is the best move for the woman in the car next to Ashford to ensure her and her child's safety?

f) In your jurisdiction, in what situations can a passenger in the vehicle be charged with impaired driving or reckless endangerment?

g) Suppose Ashford leaves a bar, realizes he's drunk, and simply gets into his car with the keys in the ignition to "sleep it off."
1. In your jurisdiction, can Ashford still be charged with driving under the influence, and if so, why?
2. If not, do you think it should be an offense? If so, why?

h) In your jurisdiction, what are your responsibilities to the police and courts if you report an impaired driver? Is it worth reporting?

The Wheel! Of! Impairment!

At the wheel, Ashley gave a mad shout,
While Ashford, sleep-starved, spun it about.
Pricey lawyers to fines,
Many lives lost (NOT MINE!!!)
Spin it? A risky gamble, no doubt!

The Wheel of Impairment is a game with no winners. All the prizes are terrible, or worse. The only way to win is not to play.

Things to think about, write about, or discuss

a) What are the signs you are too tired to drive before you start driving?

b) What are the safest and most effective actions to take if you find yourself too exhausted to drive while behind the wheel?

c) *Cannabis edibles or mellow strains to smoke are okay to use while driving. Since there isn't a standardized breath or blood test yet, it can't be detected, and you can't be charged.* Which parts of these statements are true or false? Discuss who you might endanger by driving high.

d) Suppose a person is under a doctor's care and is using prescription medication. Discuss whether and how they could be caught and charged with impaired driving, and what the risks are of not closely researching the possible effects of prescription drugs.

e) Glasses are the most common adaptive aid listed on a driver's license. What are some less common adaptive aids that certain drivers must use and are also listed on their license? Can a driver be cited for not using a required adaptive aid, including glasses?

f) What is the legally permitted blood alcohol level (BAC) in your state for someone under 21, an adult with a regular license, an adult with a commercial license (CDL), or other categories of drivers? Why is 0.00% the best goal? Can a police officer charge you with impaired driving even if your BAC is below the limit, and if so, when?

g) What effect does extreme stress have on essential driving skills like focus and reaction time? How do these effects compare to those caused by alcohol? What are some safe ways to lower stress before driving and while driving?

Avoidance technique: Mindset and Perspective II

Practice relaxation techniques to reduce stress before and during driving. Here are some simple, safe ideas for most situations. If you're uncomfortable or unsure about using these techniques while driving, do them before entering the vehicle or when you pull over for a relaxation break.

Deep breathing: Take slow, deep breaths to help calm yourself when feeling frustrated. Some recommend breathing in through your nose and then slowly out of your mouth. Short deep breathing routines with a few quick inhales and exhales, keeping your eyes open and your focus on the road, are usually fine.

Do not perform breathing exercises behind the wheel that require closed eyes or cause reduced mental focus!

Muscle relaxation: Flex and relax various muscle groups before entering the car or while safely stopped.

Use focus games: By playing focus games you may have practiced as a child (name a few things you see or hear; list the items such as the groceries in your bags, the states you have visited, or the roster of your favorite team), you can distract your mind from things that are making you anxious. *This activity should be done before driving or while the vehicle is safely stopped.*

Prayer or meditation: Depending on your belief system, practices like prayer, mindfulness, and meditation can help you relax before driving. *Any practice that requires closing your eyes, involves inward focus or detachment, or prevents full awareness of your surroundings and driving responsibility should only be done before entering the vehicle or starting the engine.*

Counting: Count from 1 to 10 before reacting to a situation, if it doesn't detract from your full focus.

Music: Listen to calming music or a relaxing playlist to boost your mood and lower stress. For some, audiobooks are just as effective or even more so than relaxing music.

- What are other safe ways you currently relax before or while you drive? What things could you try to see if they work for you?

- What other relaxation actions, like closing your eyes, taking your hands off the wheel, removing your feet from the pedals, or losing focus on your surroundings, *should you never* do *while driving*?

The Rural Railroad Rager

At the crossing, a sign warns of trains,
But Ashford, with questionable brains,
With a train rumbling near,
Ash screamed, "Put it in gear!"
While the flagman thought, "This dude's insane"

This illustration shows a rural railroad crossing without automatic gates or crossing lights. This train moves very slowly, so crossing safety staff walk ahead to warn traffic. However, consider these questions for urban environments that have faster trains, crossing gates, and signal lights.

Things to think about, write about, or discuss

a) What are some reasons Ashford believes the car in front of him should be crossing right now? Can Ash earn a citation?

b) Review the rules for railroad crossings in your area. How far must you stop from railroad tracks, whether or not there is a gate?

c) In an area with infrequently used freight railroad tracks that lack automatic gates, should you worry (or not worry) if you end up stopping on the tracks in heavy vehicle traffic? Why or why not?

d) How many feet and how much time does it typically take for a freight train to stop at the speeds they travel in your area?

e) How many feet and how much time does it typically take for a passenger train to stop at the speeds they travel in your area?

f) How many people are injured or killed each year in your state due to vehicle collisions with trains? Of these incidents, how many involved train passengers or staff, and how many involved people in vehicles?

g) Some train-vehicle collisions can be avoided if drivers follow rules and regulations. Vehicle, train, or signal equipment failures can also cause collisions. Research recent collisions. What surprised you?

h) Discuss how preventable train and vehicle collisions are. How can you ensure you avoid them?

i) What other common or uncommon vehicle and railroad safety elements should you be aware of?

The Wide Berth Bumper Buffer

Ashley blocked where the big rig would turn,
Though cars behind her showed some concern.
Ash just sat unaware,
While the trucker just glared.
The street filled with loud horns in return.

Truckers are essential to commerce and often need to navigate in tight spaces. This illustration shows an example of a wide turn that can happen in various city and town locations. Similar turns can also occur on rural roads, parking lots, and delivery zones. Be sure to follow the rules and etiquette specific to your area.

Things to think about, write about, or discuss

a) The trucker had to navigate a careful balance between swinging into the oncoming lane and "hopping" on the curb.
   1. Discuss the options and the "physics" that the truck driver experiences and how you could respond to it as a nearby driver.
   2. Is it appropriate for the truck driver to enter the opposing lane or hop a curb? And if so, when?

b) Describe Ashley's current situational awareness or lack of it. Also, describe the pedestrian's current situational awareness or lack of it.

c) What is the legality and/or etiquette of the actions of the two cars behind Ashley?

d) What types of preparation and communication (verbal, gestures, indicator signals) should happen between the truck driver and Ashley to prevent this situation? How can it be corrected when it occurs?

e) If the green traffic light allowing the truck's right turn switches to red during the maneuver, and Ashley's light turns green, how should Ashley respond?

f) What should Ashley have foreseen, and what steps should she have taken as she neared the red light?

g) Now that Ashley is in this situation, should she reverse the distance needed for the truck to pass? Is it generally legal for her to do so?

The Power Outage Panic

When the traffic lights failed in the town,
Cars at each corner were slowing down.
With the signals now dead,
Drivers filled up with dread.
A four-way stop? Don't act like a clown.

The traffic signals aren't working, and traffic is backing up. In this illustration, Car A pulled through the intersection first. Neither Car B nor Car C are indicating a turn; both want to go straight. Assume they arrived at the same time, and Car A was already in the intersection.

Things to think about, write about, or discuss

a) According to the accepted rules and regulations for this situation, should Car B or Car C go next, and why?

   In other situations, many variables must be considered. Which car arrived first? Turning directions? Which is the main road, and which is the side road? And more! Review your driver manual, other materials, and consult with instructors. For now, let's focus on the Ashes!

b) If B and C aren't sure whether the other knows the rules, and the Ashes don't know or care about the rules, what should B and C do?
   1. Use hand gestures and eye contact to clarify who proceeds next, even if B and C know or think they know the rules.
   2. Proceed when the angriest Ash looks like they'll pass illegally.

c) How should you treat a four-way intersection when traffic signals are completely out?

d) Why is confirming intentions with eye contact and hand signals almost always a good idea?

e) If this situation changed and you were the only visible car other than an Ash behind you, should you:
   a. Slowly "roll" through the intersection at less than 10 mph?
   b. Honk to warn traffic you might not have seen, then proceed?
   c. Something else?

f) If one of the Ashes knows the rules, should they be honking to tell the "correct" car to proceed?

g) How does noise and rage affect an already stressful situation in an area with the power and traffic lights out?

ROOT CAUSES OF AGGRESSIVE DRIVING

What other reasons can you identify?

Root cause: Poorly Regulated Emotions

Some people have personality traits that make them more likely to experience aggressive driving and road rage.

It is troubling and sad, but today too many people are often angry, impatient, or struggle to control their emotions.

Why would this trait change while they're driving? Why wouldn't it? Explain if it is likely that one can be poorly regulated in most situations, but remain cool as a cucumber while driving.

People who tend not to be able to "let go" of frustrating things may ruminate on them while driving and be at a higher risk of aggressive and unsafe behaviors.

These predispositions are hard to change, but not impossible to change.

Changing them benefits everyone by promoting safer driving and can give you and others a calmer driving environment and a calmer life.

The Left Lane Loiterer and Triggered Tailgaters

Ashley sped up, but Ashford stayed slow,   *In the right lane, a driver kept pace,*
The left lane was blocked, nowhere to go.   *Ashton tailgated, nose in their space.*
Ashford just stared ahead,   *But the lane's meant for slow,*
Ashley's patience, long dead,   *And with nowhere to go,*
Their hot tempers both ready to blow!   *Ashton's rage was just so out of place!*

Most people get upset when someone drives slowly or even at the posted speed limit in the passing lane. It's often the first and loudest pet peeve drivers have. There are related "Ash" issues to consider.

Things to think about, write about, or discuss

a) Discuss possible reasons why Ashford might have ended up in the passing lane but felt unsafe to move over at this exact moment.

b) Whether Ashford has a valid reason to be in the passing lane right now or not, how does Ashley's honking, tailgating, and rage affect the situation and safety?

c) Ashley was going 80 mph and is now limited to 65 mph in the passing lane. What safer, calmer alternatives does Ashley have instead of tailgating and raging?

d) Generally, how does Ashley's current driving style affect her travel time to her destinations? How does it impact her safety? And the safety of others?

e) Ashton is tailgating the car in front of him, which is already going the speed limit in the slow lane.
   1. If the car in front of Ashton "brake checked" him, what might the outcome be? Is it appropriate considering Ashton's driving?
   2. Is the car in front of Ashton required to speed up until Ashton can pass on the left?

f) Considering the other vehicles in this illustration are mostly driving reasonably, despite exceeding the posted speed limit, what kind of collision or collisions could any of Ash's actions cause? Also, how should the other cars around them adjust their positions or actions (if at all) to improve their own safety and that of others?

The Lazy Left Losers

Three stop signs are in this traffic flow.
Ashley's turn, danger clearly on show.
Ash followed – much too soon!
Driving fast, like a goon,
and these cars nearly needed a tow!

Ashley and Ashford are aggressive and dangerous here. Ashley moved into the oncoming lane on the side street while making her left turn, cutting off the car approaching the stop line. Ashford failed to take his proper turn at the three-way stop by following Ashley without waiting. He cut off the car across from him (on the top left), which stopped abruptly to avoid a collision.

Things to think about, write about, or discuss

a) Where should Ashley have been looking to get a more accurate turn that would have avoided her entering the oncoming lane?

b) How did Ashley's speed or impatience impact this scenario?

c) The car driving on the side street was going slowly as it approached the stop sign, but Ashley's visibility of the car was limited because of the buildings. Would it be Ashley's fault if there were a collision?

d) Suppose that the car in the top-left had come to a complete stop and then started to "creep" slowly over his stop line as Ashley was almost out of the intersection. Could the "creeping" be related to Ashford cutting him off? Should that car have anticipated and accepted Ashford's cutting in line, and just called it a day?

e) How could pedestrians in this scenario have influenced how drivers should have responded here, considering there are no pedestrian crossing lights, only painted crosswalks?

f) Suppose a large truck tries to make a left turn in this situation, and it is physically impossible for the truck to complete the turn onto the side street without using the side street's right lane. What actions could the car on the side street take to help the truck turn safely?

The Box Blocking Bonehead

Ash and Ashley stopped on the square lines,
Blocked the box despite obvious signs.
East and west cars did stew,
Nothing else they could do,
Besides wish a cop issued a fine.

Ashford and Ashley both are "blocking the box."

Things to think about, write about, or discuss

a) How did this happen? How could it have been prevented? Could anyone be cited for this situation?

b) What actions could the cars on the left and right sides of this illustration, the ones on the side street, take at this moment?

c) At this moment, which vehicles could get a citation in nearly all jurisdictions, and why?

d) Ashford is already blocking the box. How would law enforcement view Ashford reversing his vehicle a few feet to let traffic cross the intersection? Would it be seen as a "fix" for his current infraction or as an additional violation?

e) What rules do Ashford and Ashley need to review?

f) If there were no "don't block the box" signs and road paint, would it be acceptable for Ashley and Ashford to be where they are, in your state or municipality?

g) If active emergency vehicles need to pass through the intersection that the Ashes are blocking, what should happen?

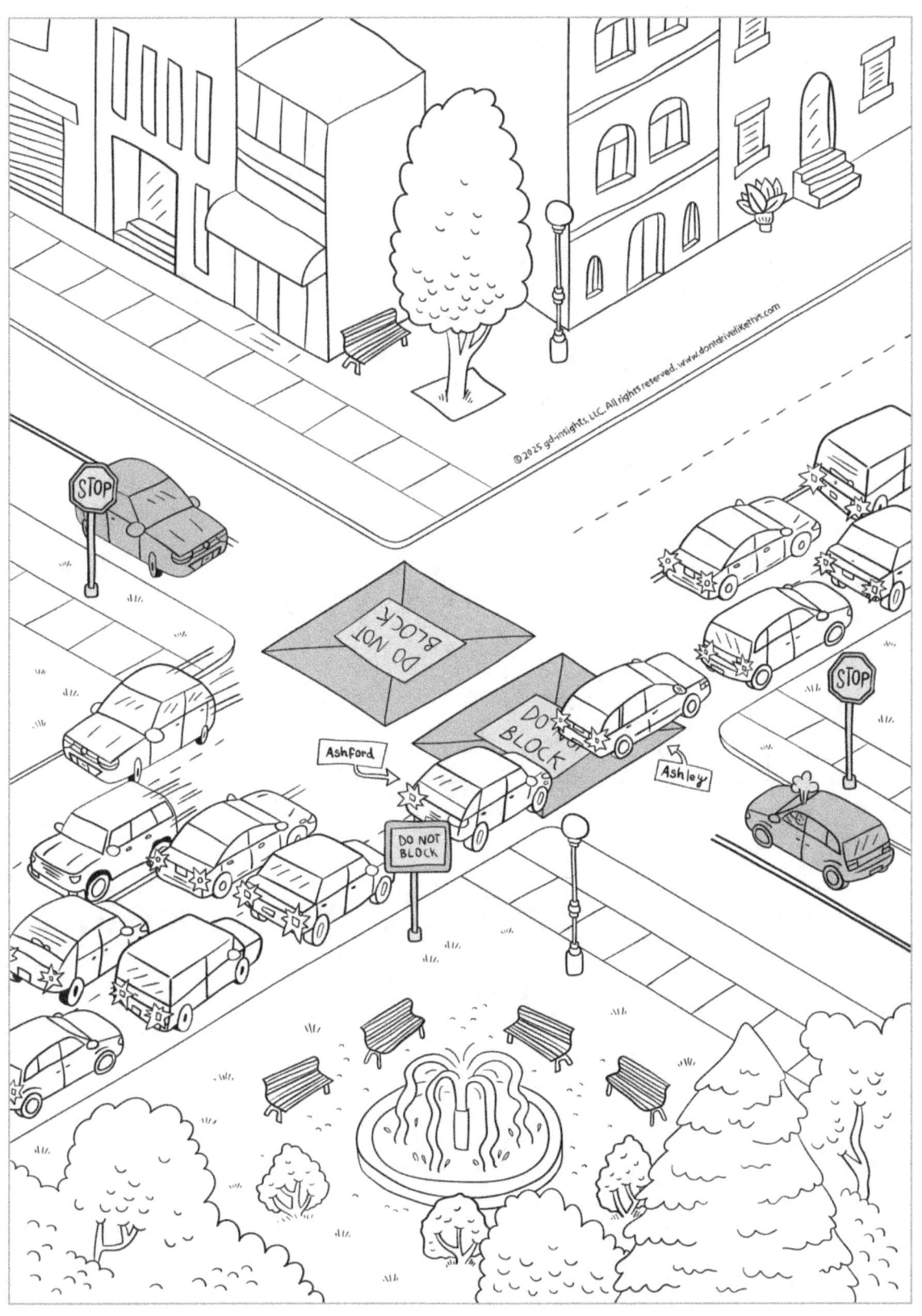

Root cause: Wild-West Road Justice

Too many drivers believe they should take on the role of teaching other drivers "a lesson." This is a misguided sense of road justice. When taken to extremes, it's clear that such behavior resembles vigilante actions.

This type of aggression, where drivers act as self-appointed punishers of others' transgressions, results in dangerous behavior for themselves and everyone nearby.

This behavior is almost always pointless, as the other driver is unlikely to learn a lesson anyway. When was the last time you learned something from someone yelling at you or approaching you aggressively, even if you were in the wrong?

This particular kind of aggressive driver is more likely to create additional danger than to address or educate others about their infractions.

Of course, the driver receiving road justice might not have done anything wrong in the first place. Ashley or Ashford could have been mistaken!

The person they're trying to teach a lesson might have no idea what our Ashes are trying to communicate to them and only perceive rage.

The Flipped Script of Win!

From "I win!" to "I care!" in a flip,
Ashford's anger replaced by a quip.
With a deep, calming breath,
He leaves rage to the rest.
Now his journeys are smooth every trip.

We are all responsible for the story of our lives. We control our scripts. Our scripts can be edited. If you recognize too many Ash-like thoughts and behaviors in your driving or, frankly, in other areas of your life, you are never too young or too old to learn and change.

How you recognize and make these changes depends on your own ethics, family background, cultural background, and abilities. Just remember, people in your situation have learned and changed before. And if you need to, you can learn new thought patterns and behaviors, too.

Things to think about, write about, or discuss

a) How can I recognize when I have thoughts and behaviors that resemble one of the Ashes?

b) What techniques and support systems will work best for me, my family, and my community to help me adjust, make necessary changes, or learn new skills?

c) How will I approach and respond to others who are acting like an Ash? How will I learn to avoid escalating aggression that others may have started and use avoidance techniques to remove myself, loved ones, and other community members from rage and potential dangers? All while not considering myself "the loser" or "a wimp?"

d) How can I define genuine "wins" on the road as calm, safe, patient, legal, and community-minded behaviors? How can I flip the script and respond differently to the thoughts and behaviors of Ashley or Ashford road rager? In our world, wins are about saving time, reducing expenses, protecting property, and saving lives—real wins, not just the fantasy "wins" of an aggressive or raging mind. Please...

Don't Drive Like an Ash!™

Avoidance Technique: You are in Control of You!

YOU, my friend, are in control of YOU. Nobody else is.

Not your parents, friends, relatives, police officers, girlfriend, teachers, boyfriend, spouse, religious leaders, internet influencers, your grandparents, the cool dude or dudette in the Lambo, politicians, or the ghost in the attic.

Nobody else is in control of your safe driving.

Just **YOU**.

YOU can commit to being a safe driver.

YOU can learn how to keep a positive attitude even in stressful situations.

YOU can use humor to keep calm.

YOU can be a role model for siblings, children, and others.

YOU can refuse to drive impaired.

YOU can reduce injuries and collisions with your attitudes and actions.

YOU can avoid aggressive driving.

YOU can change road statistics for the better.

YOU can live 'til a ripe old age.

YOU can help others live 'til a ripe old age.

Thank you in advance for helping keep yourself, your family, me, my family, and everyone else safe and happy on and around the road.

Don't Drive Like an Ash™

www.ingramcontent.com/pod-product-compliance
Lightning Source LLC
Chambersburg PA
CBHW081715120626
46550CB00010B/3143